WICCA 2000

WICCA 2000

Invocations, Prayers, and Rituals for the Magickal Millennium

Patricia Telesco

A Citadel Press Book
Published by Carol Publishing Group

A Citadel Press Book
Published by Carol Publishing Group
Citadel Press is a registered trademark of Carol Communications, Inc.

Editorial, sales and distribution, rights and permissions inquiries should be addressed to
Carol Publishing Group, 120 Enterprise Avenue, Secaucus, N.J. 07094

In Canada: Canadian Manda Group, One Atlantic Avenue, Suite 105, Toronto, Ontario
M6K 3E7

Carol Publishing Group books may be purchased in bulk at special discounts for sales
promotion, fund-raising, or educational purposes. Special editions can be
created to specifications. For details, contact: Special Sales Department,
Carol Publishing Group, 120 Enterprise Avenue, Secaucus, N.J. 07094.

Manufactured in the United States of America
10 9 8 7 6 5 4 3 2 1

Library of Congress Cataloging-in-Publication Data

Telesco, Patricia, 1960–
    Wicca 2000 : invocations, prayers, and rituals for the magickal
millennium / Patricia Telesco.
        p.   cm.
    ISBN 0-8065-2062-0 (pbk.)
        1. Witchcraft.   I. Title.   II. Title: Wicca two thousand.
BF1566.T34   1999   99-17476
299--dc21   CIP

CONTENTS

Introduction

> . . . All life is interrelated. All are caught in an inescapable
> network of mutuality, tied in a single garment of destiny.
>
> —Dr. Martin Luther King Jr.

Time marches onward, taking us collectively and individually ever
closer to destiny. In this ceaseless motion there come moments
when humankind finds itself reassessing the state of the world, let
alone the state of our hearts. The year 2000 and what lies beyond
represents one such juncture.

A review of two thousand years of chronicled history reveals
certain characteristics in our makeup and in the human state.
Actions driven by love, hate, curiosity, disbelief, or faith (just to
name a few) appear common to all people no matter the era or
setting. Among these traits, searching for our spiritual nature and
the Sacred Parent has recently resurfaced as a coping mechanism
for facing the uncertainties of our individual and collective future.

Every day, more people turn to alternative belief systems as a
way of taking control of their reality, and building a better life.
Wicca finds itself among these belief systems as one of the fastest
growing religions in the world. As a microcosm of humanity,
Wicca also finds itself going through a period of reassessment.

Wiccans believe wholeheartedly that a faith that does not grow will stagnate and die. Consequently, Wiccans try to continually adapt to the earth's and societal changes in the way they express their faith. Now that the new millennium is at our doorsteps, the need for adaptation, growth, and change is all the more clear and pressing. Yesterday's "magic" has become today's reality, and today's magic can become tomorrow's reality if we modify it and use it properly.

Humankind is about to write a whole new chapter in its spiritual journey, and Wiccans want to be an important part of the writing process. This means that we have to work to improve public understanding of the Craft, overcoming the negative or misleading stereotypes. It also means that we have to find ways to positively practice our beliefs in a "strange new world." In response to these needs, *Wicca 2000* furnishes effective techniques to welcome and live in the new millennium using potent, life-affirming magic as a tool.

Wicca 2000 also provides simple, creative ideas for transforming the way our faith is practiced, beginning today so we can build toward tomorrow. From divination, prayers, and meditations, to spells and rituals, *Wicca 2000* offers an active philosophy focused on the Sacred as a guiding force. In a world where change happens very quickly, and where people already feel uncertain about the future, this focus becomes all the more important.

Wiccans believe that the Sacred resides in everyone and everything, connecting each to each with invisible strands of energy. As we move into a new era, the extent to which we remain conscious of this network, and honor it, will determine our ability to live peaceably with one another. It will also determine our capacity to live in reciprocity with our planet and keep humankind off the endangered species list—an ability many visionaries have doubted.

Prophets, fortune-tellers, and other "seers" in nearly every historical setting made grim predictions about the millennium or the planet's future in general. Other people, who interpret the cryptic phrases of writers like Nostradamus and Edgar Cayce, seem to agree. According to students of prophesy, humankind is running headlong into certain disaster. Is this dismal outlook inevitable? Not necessarily.

As people forecast "the end times," I am reminded of many doomsdayish predictions that never came true. For early tribal societies, an earthquake or volcano might have indicated "sure" disaster. Later on, comets appearing in the sky preceded "the end." But that finality never came.

Fortunately for us, the future is not transcribed indelibly on tablets from Zion. Tampering with Mother Nature and misusing her resources began a plot whose climax *could* be bleak, but the final chapters are still being written. Wiccans believe that the predicted cataclysm can be edited or erased altogether by using positive magic, and by becoming proactively involved in efforts for change.

We, as the citizens of earth, have the capacity to create astounding wonders if we keep wisdom, foresight, love, and faith as constant companions. The future is certainly worth working toward with hope in our hearts. Thus, *Wicca 2000* looks at magic in the new millennium with similar optimism, adding preparedness and creativity as helpmates.

In those moments when you feel unsure about the future, when life's pace seems to overwhelm your faith, or when you want to help make the future something really special, turn to this inspirational guide. In it you will find hundreds of hands-on metaphysical activities to bring confidence, magic, and miracles into your reality. Adapt or add these ideas to your spiritual vision to rediscover wholeness today, and energize positive changes in personal and planetary conditions tomorrow.

WICCA 2000

1

Future Visions,
Ancient Quests

The golden age is not in the past, but in the future; not in
the origin of human experience, but in its consummate
flower.

—E. H. Chapin

Since the moment humankind recognized the inevitability of a
"tomorrow," we have looked for effective ways to peek into that
future. The methods developed to open time's window were as
diversified and unique as the eras and cultures in which they grew.
From tarot decks and dice to divining by dust, no technique that
could possibly provide insight was overlooked. Yet no matter the
approach, our ancestor's goals were similar—that of uncovering
answers to questions that could improve life's quality.

Today, divination remains a popular mystical art used by Wiccans to gain insights into the present and future. No matter our
spiritual leanings, most people are finding themselves feeling a little

antsy about the next thousand years and what they hold. This may explain, in part, why so many new tarot decks and alternative divination systems have come on the market in recent years. No matter the cause, however, the divinatory arts are uniquely suited to preparing for, and living in, rapidly transforming times. After all, many seers used divination to make their predictions about the millennium and personal futures, now it's your turn!

Omen and Sign Observance

One of the oldest and simplest methods for looking into the future is observing the present—specifically observing nature and her citizens. Wiccans feel that the world is a classroom for our spirits, and that all natural items teach valuable lessons if we're willing to take the time to watch closely. Nature also follows universal patterns and cycles, meaning that studying these can lead to valuable insights about what the future holds.

To illustrate: Trees exhibit the cycle of growth, death, and rebirth each year as the seasons change. When the trees bud early or fade late it speaks of some external influence (probably weather patterns). By observing these fluctuations regularly, and diligently noting the outcomes, one could then begin "predicting" weather patterns with greater accuracy.

Omen and sign observation is considered a passive form of divination because it's based on things over which you have no control—a bird in flight, the way the sun shines, where lightning strikes, and the like. Each of these harbingers manifests of its own accord, bringing divine or universal portents with it. While not everything that happens has significance, being alert to potential signs means you're less likely to miss things that really do hint at your future—or the world's future.

In addition to natural occurrences, I've added some technologically generated ones too. With urban sprawl becoming more and more common, people have fewer chances to observe nature other than at a zoo. Consequently, we have to modernize and adjust our omens according to the era and environment in which we live.

Signs and Omen Correspondences

Animals

Animals or animal pictures appearing in peculiar locations, at unusual times, or acting oddly often carry a message for us. For example, a squirrel running frantically *out* of a tree might presage danger in the area, as do mice leaving any region. Cats and dogs become nervous or anxious just before earthquakes or electrical storms.

To determine the meaning of an animal omen, consider the type of animal, what it's doing, and environmental conditions at the time. Traditionally activity that occurs on your left side precedes trouble, while movement to the right predicts improvements. Also check to see if any pressing questions have been on your mind recently. The animal (as a symbol) may be a direct answer to that question.

Backfires (car)

At unexpected moments, or in unusual regions, this might portend a death by shooting, or a project that could similarly "backfire" if left unattended.

Bells

When a bell tolls without human assistance, or stops without warning, especially at midnight, this predicts a regional calamity or the death of a leader nearby. On a smaller scale, this can also apply to a car horn, watch, or clock alarm. (See clocks.)

Birds

Watch the movement and type of bird for signs about your future. Seeing a black bird means good news is forthcoming. A blue bird predicts happiness, a crow indicates the need for caution, a dove represents peace, and an eagle means success is on the horizon.

Seeing a hawk, especially on your right side, portends a victory, sometimes a legal one.

Seeing an owl indicates that you're in for a mystery, red birds signify the fulfillment of a longtime wish, a bird pecking at a window warns of death, and sparrows alert you to bad prospects in love. Birds that sing at any auspicious occasion foretell unity and harmony among those gathered.

For the state of world or local affairs, entire flocks of birds arriving in an area, or leaving it suddenly, often speak of severe weather changes for boon or bane. Flying in circles, flocks may reveal the death of a leader, or an area where trouble will soon break out.

Clocks

A clock chiming at in-between hours, stopping suddenly, or its alarm going off without being set are all negative omens, usually foreshadowing a death. However, some people use the time noted when the alarm rang as "lucky" numbers for betting in the lottery.

A clock whose alarm will not cease ringing, even when turned off, warns of a situation or emotions raging out of control. As with bells, these omens may be applied to doorbells, car alarms, wristwatches, and the like.

Clouds

Observe the clouds on the evening of the Winter Solstice (December 20 approximately). If they turn black, a flood is coming in the next year. Yellow clouds precede a prosperous year, and white ones precede war.

Unusual cloud colors can act as omens at other times of the year too. Orange-tinted clouds in spring predict a plentiful harvest, but an early one. Green-tinted clouds appear before a period of prosperity or abundance, and blue-tinted clouds may indicate a peaceful end to a revolt or personal battle.

Comets

Seeing a white comet foretells a year of peace. Ones of any other color warn of hurricane, other natural disasters, or global conflicts. Some people also feel these precede the death of great leaders.

Computers

As one of the most common forms of technology, frequent computer problems may indicate more than hardware or software difficulties. For example, if you have trouble with your network server regularly, perhaps your personal communications are likewise faulty. Or, if your computer goes down a lot without any discernable cause, consider whether or not you're giving yourself enough downtime. Inaccessible files can speak of someone who's cut themselves off from others due to fear or misunderstandings.

Dreams

While dreams are driven by our subconscious, they can also bring messages to us from the spirit world and beyond. Since most people don't actively go looking for these messages, I've included them here as a passive form of omen and sign interpretation.

The number of images that *could* bear futuristic insights are as limitless as everything that ever was, or will be, part of this world. The difficult part is knowing which ones really foretell or presage future events. Some dream keys available, while over-generalized, review traditional dream omens. So, this is one place to look for insights. Also, consider if the dream seemed to have a setting, date, or other imagery that you would immediately associate with the future (like a flying car). This type of image in a dream potentially earmarks it as precognitive.

It is incredibly useful to keep a diligent log of any dream that you feel contains an omen or sign of future events (personal or global). This written record will verify or refute the validity of the foreshadowing and give you more confidence in those visions once frequent "hits" appear.

Fires

The way fires behave can foreshadow the weather and other matters. A fire that refuses to light, or one that gets blown out with
one angry gust of wind, for example, are negative omens for the
house or region in which they occur. Slow-catching fires indicate
the need for caution in a situation. Fires that spark portend forthcoming money. Those that flare up suddenly warn of arguments
while those that crackle predict an early frost. Finally, if a coal
from a fire lands at your feet, expect a terrific year.

Horns

As a type of modern bell, a horn sounding loud and long by itself
acts like a warning, either to the individual who owns the car, or
to the whole community within hearing distance. Intermittant
blaring horns predict important news.

Jets

Jets are the "birds" of today and tomorrow. Consider the color of
the jet, its direction, and any discernable words painted on its side
for more specific significance. For example, based on bird omens,
a jet with a lot of black paint moving toward you could presage
consequential news, while the same jet moving away from you
could mean you're missing an important message.

Lights

Lights going on or off by themselves, or light bulbs popping, act
as alternative sun or fire signs. For example, a light going on
during an important event could be interpreted as a positive omen
for those involved, or for whatever the event represents. A light
bulb popping, on the other hand, might be regarded as a negative
omen of exploding tempers or detrimental secrets being revealed.

Moon

A ring around the moon precedes very cold weather, possibly
accompanied by snow or ice. A red moon forecasts global prob-

lems such as war, famine, or plague. Lunar eclipses warn of global social decline.

Rainbows

Rainbows represent the promise of a better tomorrow. Half rainbows predict a fight or some type of division between people, usually among a group. Double rainbows presage a time of safety and blessing. Those appearing on a road ahead counsel that you should turn back; danger lies in that direction. Rainbows on a Saturday preface a stormy week, predominantly red ones foretell of social uprisings, and predominantly green ones prophesy a period of abundance.

Stars

In some cultures seeing a shooting star means the viewer will have many children and marry soon. If the tail of the meteor splits as it falls, this predicts improvements in human civilization over the next year.

Stereos, Radios, or Speakers

When these suddenly sound, note the first thing you hear. The words or music may have significance to situations that lay heavy on your heart and mind. Otherwise, these generally act as alternative bell signs that specifically address matters of communication. For example, rather than literal death, a speaker blaring at midnight could symbolize a parting or demise caused by loud, thoughtless words.

Sun

Because of its importance to agriculture, hunting, and other matters of human survival, the sun shining at any gathering has always been considered a sign of Divine blessing. Weddings in particular seem to benefit from this occurrence, as the shining sun represents the promise of harmony and happiness.

If the sun shines on January 25 or September 20, this predicts a year of peace and plenty for the world. Solar eclipses, on the other hand, traditionally represent very negative omens. They forewarn of global disasters, violence, and fierce weather patterns.

Thunder and Lightning

Thunder during a new moon predicts an improvement in the stock market, especially for agriculturally related goods. A storm in which lightning flashes without thunder is a negative sign, preceding border struggles that escalate into war. Lightning that flashes on your right-hand side indicates better days ahead, while that on the left predicts problems.

Traffic Bulletins

Did you ever pass one of these signs that seemed to make no sense where it was placed as you drove farther on, or ones that flash without an apparent reason? This could be a technological harbinger. In the first case whatever word or phrase appeared on the board would be indicative of the omen. A word like *stop*, for example, could be interpreted as the need to cease a project or rethink plans.

VCRs

If your VCR stops during a tape without cause, listen to the last phrase said, or look closely at the scene portrayed for signs. For example, a hijacking scene could mean some type of terrorism will occur. On a less severe level it could represent being waylaid during a trip or while working on a project.

If your VCR counter stops more than once at the same number without any discernable reason, check the numerological correspondence and interpret accordingly. For example, "666" is regarded in some circles as a sign of evil and therefore indicates problems ahead.

Wind

When a child is born with the wind blowing to the north, she is destined for success. Those born during southerly winds will have difficulties. Easterly winds bring a life of leisure, while a westerly wind predicts a life of hard work. Observe which direction the wind is blowing on the Winter Solstice to learn more about the year ahead. The east wind presages many troubles and possible global disasters, while a southerly wind predicts increasing prices. Angry, roaring winds foretell of numerous skirmishes between people, some of which may end in war.

Trust your intuition to help in recognizing which of these, when it happens, is a true omen or sign, and which is just a natural occurrence. Also, if any of these harbingers have particularly potent personal meanings, you should always consider that association first. If the omen or sign is for you (versus being a regional or global omen), the personal association often proves more accurate than anything written in books. Each person's interpertation of an omen tends to have unique points specific to that individual's experiences and outlooks. The universe uses these personal symbols to speak to our hearts more directly.

Inspiring the Prophet Within

Each of us has a latent ability to discern the future to some extent. You can predict, with a fair amount of certainty, what time you'll get up in the morning, which route you'll take to work, and so forth. This ability comes from repeated actions and cycles in our lives. What we don't realize is that *all* existence has similar patterns that interact with one another. Once we recognize that network, we can learn to follow it to its most possible outcome.

Divination systems (see examples later in this chapter) activate our spiritual vision using archetypes of human experience in symbolic form as stimulation. By focusing on these symbols we allow ourselves to reach a heightened state of awareness from which the art of prediction becomes more natural. While this ability doesn't happen overnight unless you have a natural gift for precognition, with time and practice it *can* come.

To discover the psychic within yourself, recognize that this capacity is natural. The breadth and depth of the mind's talents have barely been tapped by science. Divination tools simply provide a medium through which you can access some underdeveloped mental abilities.

Before attempting any divination system, some personal preparation techniques will improve your insight and spiritual awareness. First, make sure you have a quiet area in which to work. Play some instrumental music and burn a little mint, rose, or cinnamon incense to energize the psychic within. Second, do a quick "self check." Are you ill, tired, angry, or frustrated? If so, seriously consider putting off your efforts for when you're in a better mental "space."

If your "self check" went fine, then move on to a brief prayer or meditation. These help put you in a receptive state of mind. Breathe slowly and evenly, allowing any residual tension or mundane thoughts to flow away from you as you exhale. Visualize sparkling white light filling your entire body as you inhale. Continue this process for at least five minutes before you try any divinatory effort, adding any prayers you feel are appropriate.

At first you'll probably find this exercise difficult to master. Humans tend to think about numerous things every second of every day, juggling ideas with actions and automatic physical necessities. Now, you're retraining your mind to focus on only *one* subject—the future, and how it will show itself in symbols in the tool you've chosen. So don't get frustrated with yourself if it seems like five minutes takes *forever*—this is quite natural, and with practice the process becomes easier.

Once you complete your meditation, follow any personal rituals in using your divination device, or the instructions provided with the tool. There are literally hundreds of systems to choose from, a few of which are covered in this chapter. If you want more options, I suggest reading my book, *FutureTelling: An Encyclopedia of Divination*. It lists worldwide divination methods and implements, applications, and adaptations beyond those given herein.

Timing Divination Efforts

Some ancient mages felt that using specific timing helped divination efforts. For example, St. Agnes' Day (January 21), Midsummer's Day, and Hallows (October 31) were thought best for asking questions about love. Additionally, working during a full moon is said to improve one's natural intuitive ability.

If you wish to add special timing to your divinatory efforts, consider the moon's phase, the time of day, and the season for themes. A waxing to full moon emphasizes growth-related questions, while a waning moon represents things that seem to be fading away. A dark moon can symbolize our "darker" natures or things that seem to be at a standstill. Night is better suited to queries about hidden or secretive matters and emotions, while daytime accents concrete questions about jobs, projects, and one's line of thinking.

During the spring consult your divination system for questions about growth-related issues, love prospects, or fertility. Come summer, consult it about your energy levels, passions, and social life. Fall fortune-telling attempts might emphasize receiving insight from spirits or discerning what rewards will come from specific efforts. Finally, during the winter, ask questions about your health, perspectives, or family.

Because of today's hectic schedules, adhering to time constraints may not be possible, or even reasonable. I do not believe that one *must* follow these guidelines for success—they simply improve the outcome of your divinatory effort.

Formulating Divination Questions

Before starting any fortune-telling effort, it's important to have a question in mind, and to keep that question in mind while working with the tool. It can be as simple as providing improved insight on and an overview of current situations, or something far more detailed and specific. Visualize that question as precisely as possible for best results.

Realize, however, that each divination system has limits to how specific it can be. Those reviewed in this chapter, for example, provide midline information consisting of more than simple yes and no answers, but not a tremendous amount of detail either. If you want a more exacting system, try Tarot cards.

Scrying

The word *scry* means "to discover." Specifically, scrying is a divinatory art in which a person thinks of a question, while observing the surface of a mirror, crystal, lake, or something similar. She then watches for images to develop on that surface "to discover" the answer to her question.

In earlier times people believed the images within a crystal, mirror, or other properly prepared surface, were caused by an indwelling spirit. In order to contact this spirit some rather elaborate rituals developed, some of which detailed things like what type of stand and cloth to use for successful results. This concept came from an even earlier tradition called animism in which people felt all of nature housed spirits that could be called upon for aid.

Modern Wiccans are not as superstitious as our ancestors. We believe that the process of careful scrutiny helps encourage a trancelike state. From this state, a person may receive symbolic or literal pictures from the collective unconscious or the Source, depending on personal beliefs. Either way, scrying is respected as a spiritual aid for gaining insight or foresight, and it is a technique that you can learn fairly easily.

Two user-friendly approaches and interpretive values for you to try follow.

Surface Scrying

For this you will need a shiny or mirrored surface such as that provided by a polished or tumbled stone, a blank TV or computer screen, the back of a spoon, or a dark-bottomed bowl of water. You might want to try all of these at least once—or try all those to which you have regular access—to find which one works best for you.

Many people find the blank TV or computer screen particularly useful. While you might scoff at the idea of hovering over these like a gypsy, your mind already expects images to appear on these surfaces. This expectation improves the probability of experiencing successful scrying sooner than you might with other media (like a spoon) where your mind does not expect to see a picture.

In any case, pick out one medium and sit it in front of you. If using a polished stone, put it against a dark surface. Meditate using the above method (page 12) or one from your own spiritual path. Concentrate on your question, then open your eyes.

Don't look directly at the object or surface. Instead try to look slightly beyond it, allowing your vision to blur a little. Continue breathing evenly, and watch. Most people find it takes some time and practice before they receive images.

When pictures do appear they can be in literal or symbolic form. Literal responses are less frequent, as these have to be nearly three-dimensional and detailed, whereas symbolic images act like the mind's shorthand. Write down whatever you see, including the shape, color, and motion of images. Decide what each vision's shape is—just as you might interpret an ink blot.

Following will be a brief list of some of the images that commonly appear and their interpretive value or meaning. Note that when a color or shape combines with movement it can change the value of that image. For example, a green cloud moving to the left could portend a financial decrease or time of scarcity. A red heart moving down could indicate decreasing passion in a relationship or lessened self-love.

SURFACE SCRYING SYMBOLIC CORRESPONDENCES

Black images: a period of rest or possible negativity

Blue images: peace, tranquility, and reason for hope

Brown images: put down foundations before proceeding

Circle: the cycles in your life, either those starting or ending—
alternatively, the circle of family or friends in which you travel

Clouds moving down: a decrease of some kind or "no"

Clouds moving left: a negative omen or "no"

Clouds moving right: a positive omen or "yes"

Clouds moving up: an increase or improvement of some kind or
"yes"

Cup: a lunar symbol that speaks of personal instincts and intuitive
senses

Flame shape: anger or other heated emotions

Green images: bright green portends prosperity or growth;
yellowish-green predicts problems caused by jealousy or an
overactive ego.

Heart: matters of love or intense emotions

Knife or scissor shape: something or someone being cut off from
you; separation

Lightbulb shaped: an idea; secrets revealed; an awakening

Orange images: a positive sign; the harvest of your labors

Pentagram: a focus on the mystical or the need for protection

Purple images: a focus on spirituality is needed or increased awareness of your leadership abilities

Red images: intense feelings like anger or passion that affect the
outcome of your situation

Rings: a forthcoming engagement or marriage announcement

Square: the need for stability or an improved awareness of earth

Star: wishes fulfilled; an elevated status

Sun: a positive omen of blessing and improvements

Triangle: three-way situations, for boon or bane

Yellow images: bright yellow indicates renewed creativity that
brings success; mustard yellow is indicative of illness (mental or
physical) that hinders progress

If you see images or shapes other than those given here, consult a tea-leaf reading book, dream symbol key, or other collection of symbolism for ideas on interpretive values.

Fire Scrying

For this you need a fire source such as a long-handled match, a candle, brazier, or fireplace. For safety reasons I do not recommend trying this with a lighter, however. If using a match you will also need a holder (like those for incense) and a fireproof surface on which to put the two. If using a candle, consider dabbing thyme oil on it to encourage psychism. If using a brazier or fireplace, add a little lemongrass for similar effect.

Once the fire is burning, use a scrying process like you used for surfaces. You may see colors, shapes, and images form within the coals or flames. The fire's tongues, and the smoke generated, provide additional symbols for consideration. In esoteric traditions, these responses are thought to be generated by an elemental creature called a Salamander, who lives passionately and joyfully as long as the fire does.

Following is a brief list of potential fire signs. For alternative values look for a good book on pyromancy.

FIRE AND SMOKE SYMBOLIC CORRESPONDENCES

Blazing suddenly: problems on the horizon, often caused by a person unknown to you

Bluish flames throughout: the presence of spirits or a forthcoming storm (figurative or literal)

Bright flames that slowly increase: a positive omen—move forward confidently

Circular sparks: financial improvements

Dying suddenly: a negative omen of something that ends before completion

Fire won't catch: a very negative omen—do not proceed

Singular flame peak: single-mindedness aids your goal

Smoke, dark and dense: a negative omen, especially if it hovers over the fire

Smoke dividing: feeling torn between two equally appealing options or a separation of some kind

Smoke moving due east: the ability to overcome forthcoming trouble; the harvest that comes from diligent work

Smoke moving due north: don't continue until you've put foundations under your dreams or goals

Smoke moving due south: don't let your emotions, especially anger, rule your actions

Smoke moving due west: the ability to overcome a problem if you let your heart guide you

Smoke moving left or down: a negative omen—proceed with caution

Smoke moving right or up: a positive omen—move ahead with hope in your heart

Smouldering: hostility and resentment cause problems

Split flames: a division; a lack of unity

Three flame peaks: the need for help from friends, or to focus more on your triune being (body-mind-spirit)

Tiny sparks: personal loss, often money-related

If you have the opportunity to try fire scrying outdoors at a bonfire, all the better. The backdrop of flame becomes like a big screen TV to watch for images. As you observe, let the motion and warmth of the fire wrap you in energy, deepening your level of sensitivity to its messages.

Lot Casting

The phrase "The die is cast" owes its inception to the ancient art of lot casting. Ancient people cast lots using dice, beans, and other small objects. The outcome of these castings determined many things from forecasting a battle's success and elected leaders to resolving inheritances and even choosing a prisoner's sentence.

Try lot casting yourself. First determine the medium and find a suitable medium for it. I suggest choosing a durable medium like dried colored beans, colored popcorn kernels, game board dice or tokens, runes, wood slices, or nuts and bolts. Also, locate a piece of soft, natural cloth that measures as least 12" × 12" and draw a good-sized circle on it.

Some cast systems, like runes, have specific interpretive values already assigned. If you're putting together a personalized collection (see Household Objects, this section), I suggest having at least five tokens. Each additional token increases the randomness of a reading and the potential interpretive value. I actually work with fifteen objects, but some may find this cumbersome.

No matter the medium you've chosen, it's important to predetermine what each token in the set means, and if that meaning will change depending on where the token lands. Make notes of the associations to maintain congruity from reading to reading. While the consideration and notation process take a little time, it is well worth the effort. The more you ponder and refine your divination tool, the better you will understand it, and the better it will work for you.

Hold the symbolic tokens you've chosen in a bowl or bag over the casting surface. Shake them thoroughly with your eyes closed while thinking of a question. After a few moments of thought, randomly release a few, or all, of the objects to the surface of the cloth. Anything that falls outside the circle is not interpreted.

Generally speaking, objects that land close to you represent present concerns, pressing matters, or close family and friends. Those farther away from you in the circle represent future situations, actions, or acquaintances. Things on the right are more positive omens, while those landing on the left are negative, but this only applies if you've set up your casting circle using these associations.

Lot casting is a very flexible art, being limited only by what you have on hand, your ability to relate to symbolic items, and your imagination. I personally increase the divinatory value of my casting circle by using the traditional correspondences for the four directions, for example. North represents things that are frozen, halted, or in a holding pattern. It can also symbolize the need for letting a matter rest and the winter season. East represents things that are just beginning and a time of renewed hope. On a time line, east can represent the present or following spring. South represents situations or feelings that are highly energized. It also symbolizes summer. Finally, west represents the emotional, intuitive self, and the season of fall.

When tokens land on or near these points, I adjust the interpretation accordingly. For example, an object symbolic of love that lands in the north would then represent a relationship that's going nowhere, or progressing more slowly than you like. If the same token landed in the east, it would portend the beginning of a new, or refreshed, relationship, possibly in spring.

Following are two types of lot casting.

Household Objects

People laugh at me when I tell them that some of my best casting tools come out of the kitchen junk drawer, but it's really true. There is a treasure trove of symbolic objects from which to choose around your living space. It's also a good way to recycle odds and ends into a spiritual application for the new millennium!

Exactly what you have available, and what each object represents to you, may differ from the following assortment and suggested interpretations, so don't be afraid to get creative.

HOUSEHOLD OBJECT CASTING CORRESPONDENCES

Aluminum foil scrap: being protected to some degree, but not so much that safety is guaranteed

Battery: personal energy increasing or decreasing

Bottle cap: a secret revealed for boon or bane

Bow: a pleasant surprise or gift

Bulb (Christmas style): an idea or inspiration whose outcome may be predicted by the other objects in the casting

Button with saying: matters of communication—what's written on the button may provide more insight

Checker piece: strategy—think before you act

Coin: finances—if heads, a positive omen; if tails, a negative sign (although this can be changed by nearby objects in the reading)

Comb: put things in order; the need to organize

Crayon: the child within—have you been getting enough playtime?

Dinosaur key chain: hanging on to outmoded ideas or behaviors

Egg (chocolate): something hidden beneath a shiny exterior that may, or may not, live up to promises

Film negative: looking at something the wrong way, or with too much negativity—step back and get an alternative perspective

Fingernail clipper: cut away what you don't need so you can experience real growth

Fuse, burnt out: scattering your efforts in too many places—find a singular focus and follow it through.

Key: an opportunity opens up, or the solution to a problem presents itself

Magnet: attracting specific energies to yourself (remember like draws like—so stay upbeat)

Matches: put a fire under projects that you've put off or given up on; alternatively a sign of warmth or passion in your future

Nail: finally tackling a difficult situation the right way (hitting the nail on the head); alternatively, a desire for security

Needle: repair a situation or relationship that's gone unattended or started to unravel

Nut in shell: fertility, especially for a man (note that this pertains to matters of creativity, knowledge, money, instead of literal fertility); alternatively a crazy (nutty) idea whose time has come

Pacifier: trying to find substitutes for what you really want rarely satisfies

Paper clip: associations with people or situations that may need strengthening

Plug, three-way: connections that require the help of friends, family, or an acquaintance to secure effectively

Rubber band: the need to stretch, grow, and remain flexible

Screw: time to stop pussy-footing around and grow a backbone—if someone hasn't been doing their fair share, say so!

Shell: the need to "go with the flow" and get in closer contact with your intuitive self

Spring: improved outlooks and an upbeat attitude will literally
    return the "spring to your step"
Stone: the need to live more simply, keeping one foot in reality
String, knotted: the web of fate or destiny, some of which is start-
    ing to reveal itself
Twist tie: keep your relationships fresh; preserve them with love,
    understanding, and constant tending
Umbrella (paper, decorative): the need to get out of some unfavor-
    able "weather" in a situation or relationship—the thing you think
    will protect you, won't
Velcro: make sure you're holding on to the right things
Wire: finding an equitable balance between rigidity and flexibility;
    alternatively, a precarious situation

Say you focus on a question regarding career changes. Upon
shaking the bowl or bag in which your tokens lie, the film, coin
(heads up), and checker fall out close to you in the circle, just to
the left of center. The key falls out midcircle near the plug, to the
right of center. This casting might represent the fact that your
financial future looks hopeful, but you've been going at things the
wrong way. You need to reconsider your job search before continuing. Once you find a different approach, the right opportunity
will open up thanks to a friend or acquaintance.

If you added the four directional markers to your cloth, the
interpretation might change slightly. In this case, a coin (heads up)
in the east would indicate positive financial changes sometime in
spring. If combined with a paperclip in the north, I'd say those
changes will come from staying right where you are. The grass
isn't always greener on the other side!

Dice Casting

Most people have three die at home or can get them easily. Dice
are also very portable, so they make a good medium for new millennium magic. In casting dice, the number of the outcome deter-
mines the query's answer instead of where it lands (see household
objects).

To begin, put the three die in a container. Shake this while thinking of a question then cast all three onto the cloth. Add together those that land within the circle, then interpret the sum as follows:

DICE CASTING CORRESPONDENCES

3: Good news, an announcement, or a gift
4: Bad news, trouble, or hindrances
5: Rejoicing; a desire is realized successfully
6: Sadness, often caused by misfortune or defeat
7: Frustration, brought on by financial difficulty or gossip
8: Miscommunication that could escalate into an argument
9: Harmony among people; a tense situation gets settled
10: Opportunity presents itself
11: Estrangement; a decrease in feelings toward a situation or person
12: Revelation, often disclosed by the media or friends
13: Melancholy; an ominous feeling that you can't shake and should probably pay attention to
14: New friends or colleagues
15: Slow down—someone isn't being totally honest
16: Adventure, possibly a trip abroad
17: Success, but one that comes from altering your tactics and approaches
18: A very positive omen; good fortune and plenty

One way to make dice lots similar to other casting methods is to cast the dice in a circle that has four to twelve symbolic tokens around the perimeter. Then, both the number showing on the die and the token near which it lands provide additional interpretive value. For example, if the sum was three and the dice landed close to a heart, you could interpret this to mean a happy love affair.

If you want some alternative interpretive values for your system, look for a good book on numerology or cleromancy (divination by dice) in the library. Both offer ideas on what each number can potentially symbolize in your reading.

Cards

Rather than being cast, cards are purposefully shuffled with the question in mind, then drawn to determine the answer to a question. For card divination, most people get a tarot deck or regular playing cards, but other options exist. Business cards, greeting cards, flash cards, or hand-drawn symbolic cards are functional media for the new millennium.

Tarot cards and playing cards already have some interpretive values ascribed to them by tradition. If you make other card sets, I recommend making at least thirteen cards so that the responses can somehow touch on the diversity of human experience. You'll also need to predetermine each card's meaning (both upright and reversed), as you did with the personally devised casting systems.

The number of cards drawn for a reading varies from system to system, so it's really up to you. I suggest minimally drawing three cards, the first of which represents the past or underlying influences. The next symbolizes present factors in the question and the final card is the future or action card. If you decide to draw more cards consider some traditional tarot or rune layouts for the designated meaning of each.

Following are two examples of card divination for you to try, expand, or adapt.

Playing Cards

Playing cards are the modern relative of tarot decks in a simplified form. Having 52 instead of 72 cards, the four major suits correspond to the four main symbols in tarot (hearts being cups, spades being swords, diamonds being coins, and clubs being rods). And, as with the tarot, each suit has an associated theme—hearts represent love and emotions, spades refer to conflicts or difficulties, diamonds are money related, and clubs focus on concrete matters, like business.

For new millennium magic, ease of use, portability, and cost are all factors in choosing divination systems. This makes playing cards an all-around winner—no one will give you a second glance for playing a unique game of solitaire, and most decks cost under five dollars!

Purchase a deck that has a definite right-side up when you look at it (in other words you can tell when the picture on the card is upside down). This increases the potential interpretive values from 40 to 80 outcomes. Next, take out all the face cards and jokers. This leaves you with ace through ten in each suit.

Shuffle the deck while thinking intently about your question, draw three cards, then interpret them according to the following generalized list. This list gives the upright meaning first, and the reversed meaning second.

PLAYING CARD CORRESPONDENCES

Hearts

Ten: *upright*—success despite difficulties
         reversed—success, but only after a long, diligent struggle

Nine: *upright*—reason for hope
         reversed—relying on the wrong person

Eight: *upright*—fondness returned
         reversed—unrequited love

Seven: *upright*—harmonious relationship
         reversed—disruptions

Six: *upright*—improvements
         reversed—unexpected turn for the worse

Five: *upright*—good counsel from a friend
         reversed—listen to your heart instead of others opinions

Four: *upright*—a move or personal transition; stay put—stop
         looking elsewhere for what you already have

Three: *upright*—problems erupt
         reversed—difficulty leads to arguments an separation

Two: *upright*—abundance, often financial
         reversed—monetary improvements that need to be handled
         prudently

Ace: *upright*—good news
         reversed—mixed or enigmatic news

Spades

Ten: *upright*—a saddening announcement
       reversed—bad news of a personal nature
Nine: *upright*—terrible situations
       reversed—death or an unhappy ending
Eight: *upright*—don't move forward with plans right now
       reversed—the destruction of efforts or plans
Seven: *upright*—small miscommunications
       reversed—misunderstanding leads to disagreement
Six: *upright*—a turnaround of some kind
       reversed—things will go downhill
Five: *upright*—troubled times, but family or friends help
       reversed—close acquaintances jump ship when trouble arises
Four: *upright*—a partnership's showing signs of trouble
       reversed—dissolution
Three: *upright*—feeling unhappy or unfulfilled
       reversed—neglect causes a separation
Two: *upright*—lies and underhandedness
       reversed—betrayal by a trusted friend or companion
Ace: *upright*—diversion from a conflict
       reversed—pleasure that results in trouble or an argument

Diamonds

Ten: *upright*—a new home or apartment
       reversed—look closely before making a contractual
         commitment
Nine: *upright*—postponement of plans by choice
       reversed—things that you cannot control cause delays
Eight: *upright*—improved finances help a relationship
       reversed—a relationship whose focus is wrong (as in money)
Seven: *upright*—spend a little money to get away from it all
       reversed—be prudent in your travels or use of vacation time
Six: *upright*—improvements
       reversed—improvements, but ones that take a lot of hard work
         to achieve
Five: *upright*—a business prospect solidifies
       reversed—be wary before accepting a forthcoming proposal
         (read the fine print)

Four.   *upright*—a raise or promotion
        reversed—carefully consider this opportunity, it may not be
           as good as it looks
Three   *upright*—legal costs
        reversed—an unscrupulous legal arrangement
Two: *upright*—a partnership blossoms potentially into love
        reversed—watch any dealings with companions closely—
           they may have hidden motives
Ace: *upright*—financial news
        reversed—good if upright, bad if reversed.

Clubs

Ten: *upright*—success, especially financial
        reversed—be wary of perceived improvements; they won't last
Nine: *upright*—a gift or offer of assistance
        reversed—accept this knowing strings are attached
Eight: *upright*—help from an acquaintance leads to prosperity
        reversed—an offer that doesn't produce what it promises
Seven: *upright*—advancement (mental, spiritual, or financial)
        reversed—fooling yourself into believing things are better
Six: *upright*—mastery of some type
        reversed—being a know-it-all instead of listening
Five: *upright*—mingling with others provides good ideas
        reversed—don't listen too closely to well-intended advice
           without listening to your heart.
Four: *upright*—disillusionment or dissatisfaction
        reversed—consider your own actions—they're causing most
           of the problem
Three: *upright*—discord followed by resolution
        reversed—discord leading to separation
Two: *upright*—watch your purse strings and allocate time carefully
        reversed—don't throw caution to the winds—stay focused
Ace: *upright*—prosperity in business
        reversed—temporary business improvements followed by
           setbacks

Say you asked about love prospects. The three cards that
appeared, in order, were the ten of spades, eight of clubs, and eight

of hearts, all upright. This could be interpreted to mean that you've been burned in past relationships. This negative experience is somehow affecting the way you act in present settings, especially with someone currently showing interest. If you let go of the past and open your eyes, you'll see that a good opportunity is waiting from which a very satisfying relationship could develop.

Please note that other interpretations for playing cards exist in various books on cleromancy if you want to personalize or adapt this system. Also, you could use the interpretive values for each card's corresponding tarot card instead, which would provide more detailed responses. Again, use your instincts to guide you in how to best decipher and apply your readings.

Greeting Cards

This is another fun way to recycle and make a divination system that really sings with the voice of your spirit. Keep all the greeting cards you get for an entire year. Go through them and separate the cards into same-size piles. Use the pile with the most cards for your deck.

Cut the front of the cards off (the side with the picture). Cover these with art spray for longevity. Look at the cards one at a time. What words or phrases come immediately to mind with the imagery? Use these as a foundation for your interpretations. For example, bells might represent announcements or joyous occasions. Reversed they could symbolize plans that go awry. Other common imagery that appears on cards can potentially be interpreted as follows:

GREETING CARD CORRESPONDENCES

Baby: *upright*—a new beginning or literal birth
            reversed—delays in getting something started
Bow: *upright*—a gift or other pleasant surprise
            reversed—a surprise that turns out badly
Boxes: *upright*—look beyond the surface to find your treasure
            reversed—a proverbial Pandora's box opening

Boy: *upright*—a young man who is helpful and kind
 reversed—a young man with his own agenda
Cake: *upright*—cause for celebration
 reversed—don't get greedy or overconfident
Cat: *upright*—curiosity leads to further mystery
 reversed—a setback, but one from which you recover
Comics: *upright*—your humor is an ally and a coping mechanism
 reversed—don't become the class clown
Dog: *upright*—faithfulness among friends and family
 reversed—dishonesty or disloyalty
Fairy: *upright*—follow your dreams wherever they lead
 reversed—keep one foot in reality when making plans
Flowers: *upright*—beauty and hope surround you
 reversed—take care; things don't "smell" right here
Fruit: *upright*—rewards that come by your own handiwork
 reversed—being undone through lack of effort
Garden: *upright*—a project comes to fruition
 reversed—delays and entanglements
Get Well: *upright*—take a break before you get sick
 reversed—unrecognized or untreated disease or illness
Girl: *upright*—a young woman who is helpful and kind
 reversed—a young woman with her own agenda
Heart: *upright*—improved love prospects
 reversed—deteriorating love prospects
House: *upright*—a new residence or job
 reversed—travel and the gypsy spirit
Ice: *upright*—progress is halted temporarily
 reversed—a standstill over which you have no control
Man: *upright*—a man who is helpful and kind
 reversed—a man with his own agenda
Moon: *upright*—listen to your instincts and trust your heart
 reversed—your intuition is faulty, get counsel
Snow: *upright*—cooling of emotions, not of your choosing
 reversed—distance yourself to get perspective
Sun: *upright*—blessings, abundance, good prospects
 reversed—temper good news with prudence and wisdom
Trees: *upright*—put down your roots to withstand the wind
 reversed—you're on dubious ground; watch your step!

Woman: *upright*—a woman who is helpful and kind
             reversed—a woman with her own agenda

Write down each card in your set and the meanings you've
given it in upright and reversed position. Shuffle and think about
your question then draw out the cards. Returning to your earlier
question about love using the list above, say you pulled the woman
(reversed), sun, and heart (reversed), in order. This might mean
that in the past a particular woman influenced the way you think
about relationships in a negative way. While right now things are
going smoothly, love's path will remain difficult in the future
unless you shake off that influence.

Children and Divination

Children have an innate ability to see beyond surface reality. Many
naturally sense the presence of spirits, for example. With this in
mind, children can use divination systems to provide them with
increased options and perspectives while growing up. While some
people might hesitate to teach a child such things, our children's
spiritual natures need to be acknowledged and encouraged. They
are, after all, our future.

Generally, children around the age of ten comprehend what
they're looking at in simple divination systems. Stone or rune sets,
in particular, seem to attract interest and attentiveness. Additionally,
because a child can play with these without fear of damage, she
can easily transfer the energy of a question into the stones.

The archetypes of the runes may still prove a little complex for
this age group, so I suggest using stones with simple, hand-painted
emblems, or a collection of various crystals instead. In either case,
the child should determine ahead of time what each stone will
mean when he pulls or casts it. Have the child consider the stone's
color, shape, where it was found, or how it feels to him to determine the associations. If this process proves difficult, a premade set
of stones call the *Sacred Stone Oracle* comes with a casting cloth,

pouch, interpretive pamphlet, and a reasonable price tag. It is available through Blue Pearl (1-800-822-4810).

An alternative type of divination that works for visually inspired children is that of reading shadow patterns. For example, when sunlight filters through the trees, it creates a pattern on the ground or on a wall in the house. Children can think of a question, then "hunt" for the images in the shadow for answers. Warning: This is not a good exercise for children who are afraid of the dark, as it may increase the instances of seeing scary images. For other children, however, I've found it to be a very productive exercise.

Divination in the New Millennium

Some divination systems have changed with the times, and others have remained timeless. Today, as we grow and move forward spiritually, we will likely find a similar trend. Some of our fortune-telling methods will transform to mirror societal changes while the archetypes in other methods will endure as tributes to humankind's communal mind and experiences. Wiccans welcome and honor both the old and the new with hopeful eyes.

All in all, I believe you'll find your divinatory efforts—today and tomorrow—fun and very rewarding. You'll notice that the accuracy increases the longer you use any system, which naturally produces more spiritual self-confidence. This assurance can then be applied to living more fully, more in tune with the Sacred, and more magically every day, thereby building a terrific future.

2

Prayer

Every tomorrow has two handles. We can take hold of it with the handle of anxiety or the handle of faith.

—H. W. Beecher

The custom of prayer has become almost passé, being replaced by the six o'clock or eleven o'clock news. With the pace of our lives showing no signs of slowing down, I fear this trend might continue if left to its own. The result? Tomorrow's spirituality could easily become like a drive-through restaurant, providing only momentary satisfaction and questionable sustenance. By reinstating prayer as part of our daily routines we invite the Sacred to provide that missing healthy spiritual fulfillment.

But what exactly is prayer? John Bunyan, an English religious authority of the 1600s, felt that prayer was "a sincere, sensible, affectionate pouring out of the soul to God." Phillips Brooks, an American Bishop of the 1800s, felt that prayer was "merely a wish turned God-ward." Victor Hugo felt that what constituted prayer depended on the attitude of one's thoughts, while Emmerson felt it was "a study of truth."

In considering these and other philosopher's views, it becomes apparent that prayer is one means of opening ourselves to the Divine in total honesty. In these moments there are no façades, no pretense—only us and our vision of god. The prayer silently or verbally sends out energy in the form of a wish, anticipating some type of answer.

Prayers can also be a form of worship. Instead of asking for something, this type of prayer uplifts the Sacred and honors its power. In these moments we reassess our connection with the God/dess, our blessings, and we acknowledge this Power's role in those blessings.

In all its forms, however, prayer reopens the lines of communication between ourselves and Spirit, resulting in a natural side effect. It generates hope and confidence—two powerful types of magic in their own right. So, if divination provides positive insights for the new millennium, prayer then provides the best possible attitude. Additionally, prayer entreats the Great Spirit to guide and enrich our spiritual path, no matter what the future holds.

Praying Effectively

How does one pray effectively? Alexander Maclaren, a Scottish theologian of the 1800s, tells us that "the prayer that begins with trustfulness and passes on into waiting will always end in thankfulness, triumph, and praise." Unfortunately, the simple beauty of these words doesn't really help when prayers are not answered as we hoped, or at all. The Great Spirit has a complete view of how an answered prayer will affect life's network. When our manifested wishes or desires would prove harmful in some way, the Divine steps in to positively reroute the prayer's energy, resulting in a different effect.

While this explanation is oversimplified at best, it is one that even Socrates advocated when he said, "God knows what is good for us." I might presume to extend his insightful words with, "even when we don't." This is why many Wiccans use the phrase "for the greatest good and it harm none" in spellcraft, ritual, and prayer. It releases the energy generated by our efforts into very capable hands.

Jeremey Taylor, an English Bishop of the 1600s, gave us more food for thought when he said, "whatsoever we beg of God, let us also work for it." This brings us back to the aphorism of God/dess helping those who help themselves. Our actions (or inactions) after prayer play a part in whether or not we get an answer. This rule of thumb keeps us actively participating in our own present and future well-being, instead of always expecting some external force to "fix" problems.

SIX STEPS TO EFFECTIVE PRAYER

1. Develop, renew, or revitalize your faith.
2. Meditate on your request and its implications.
3. Find words with which to express yourself comfortably.
4. Make practical efforts that mirror your prayer's intent.
5. Diligently and sincerely continue to pray with trust and expectation in your heart.
6. Be thankful when your prayer is answered.

In order to pray then, our first step is to have trust and faith. Without a core of belief in Greater Powers and Their wisdom, prayer becomes a rote action without consequence. Second, consider what you want to ask and think seriously about the ramifications of that request. For example, asking for rain to end a drought is different than asking for sunshine so you can go swimming. The first request serves the entire planet. The second is selfish and seeks to alter global weather patterns for personal gain. While I believe that we can (and should) pray for things we *want*, it's more important to pray for those things that we, others, or the world really *need*.

Third, use words that are comfortable on your lips, and wholly meaningful to you. While you might have the prayers from your youth memorized, they probably won't do much good unless they hold profound meaning for you. The God/dess cares about what we feel in our hearts, not fancy wording. John Bunyan provided insight on this concept when he said, "in prayer it is better to have a heart without words, than words without a heart." This bit of advice applies to all the prayers in this chapter too. Change the names of the Divine to those from your personal pantheon. Change the specifics to those more suited to your circumstances. Most importantly, reword the prayers so they truly sing the song of your soul.

Fourth, take positive action toward making the vision of your prayer a reality. If you pray for world peace, begin by making peace with yourself and your neighbors. If you pray for a job, start looking for one. Other than the occasional miracle, the most impressive results from prayer come when we act as cocreators of our destiny, taking divine guidance in one hand and self-motivation in the other.

Fifth, pray frequently, diligently, and sincerely. Allow your faith to reach out and begin the process of change for a better tomorrow. Repeat your prayers as often as you feel the need. Watch and wait with a patient, trusting, expectant heart. It may take time before a specific prayer is answered in some manner, but answers do come.

Seasonal Prayers

Let our days begin and end with God.

—William E. Channing

As the annual wheel turns, Wiccans honor earth's cycles with rituals, spells, and prayers. We do this to bring ourselves into closer harmony with nature and the universe. As time's wheel also marches forward, this harmony becomes increasingly important.

We cannot lose sight of the Earth Mother and her needs in serving our own, now or in the future.

Seasonal prayers reflect the changes in the earth, and the theme generated by those changes. Spring, for example, is a time of renewal and vitality so the prayer given at that time reflects those themes. This approach blends nature's energies with prayer to begin generating specific transformations in and around your life. By continuing to pray through and with these cycles, the process of personal change likewise continues, building the foundation for a better tomorrow.

I've kept the following seasonal prayers somewhat short, anticipating that most Wiccans will want to add them to rituals, spells, and other observances, or extend them through personalization.

Spring

Spring's theme centers on earth's renewal, so consider those things you want to restore or revitalize in your own life. All around the earth is budding with new life. If you have been considering having a child, now is an excellent time to pray for that blessing. Thanks to the ever-whimsical spring winds, this is also the perfect season to ask for help in gaining new perspectives, refreshed outlooks, and an improved sense of humor.

Spring is a season for planting. Ask yourself what types of seeds of character you want to plant in your heart so they blossom by fall. Pray for help in tending and cultivating these attributes with loving care.

A spring prayer: *Great Lord and Lady, thank you for the life you have brought once again to the earth. As your magic touches the world, plants blossom, the sap in trees begins to run, animals bear young, and the entire planet sings with joy. Let this vibrant energy all around me also energize my spirit.*

Wherever ice dams the flow of love between me and another, let it melt beneath the sun. Wherever snow hides a problem, reveal and resolve it. Where there has been illness, replace it with health. Where dark clouds linger, bring hope. Help my heart and soul blossom anew like a fresh blade of grass, reaching ever toward the light. So be it.

Summer

Summer's theme is one of abundance: abundant flowers, abundant creativity, abundant energy. As the sun reaches high in the sky, it represents the fire of passion within us, so begin focusing on prayers for improved, sensitive, sexual expression. This same light also helps us see things clearly, so pray for insight into perplexing situations. Finally, in Wiccan traditions the summer months are considered lucky so pray for improved fortune.

A summer prayer: *Lord of the Sun, thank you for warming the soil to bring forth earth's bounty. As the flowers and fruits grow to fullness around me, likewise mature the fruits of my spirit. As you burn brightly in the summer sky, so, too, burn in my heart and soul.*

Wherever a relationship has grown cool, bring warmth. Wherever secrets dwell, let them be revealed. Wherever any lingering darkness hides, chase it away with brilliant light. Let the embers that embody you ignite in me a love-based passion: for my job, for my art, for my mate, for just causes, for all that is my life. So be it.

Fall

Fall's theme is the harvest of your own labors and loves. The seeds that you planted with prayer in the spring are now ready to be reaped. Be thankful for that and for the earth's plenty.

As the sun's light slowly starts to wane, it gently reminds us that this plenty must be offset with prudence. Ask the God/dess to teach you the value of caution and foresight. Also consider renewing your attention toward any skill and pray for continued growth in that area. The energies of autumn accent mastery.

A fall prayer: *Mother of Creation, thank you for your bounty. All around the earth has grown to maturity. So too, I pray, may I see signs of my own maturity. Help me to recognize the progress in my spirit, to see the fruits of character and insight that have developed since spring. Let me hold those gifts close to my heart as sacred and special.*

As I move into fall, teach me balance. Let me know the wonders of both sounds and silences, rest and action, the temporal and spiritual. As I walk the Path of Beauty, keep my eyes on the horizon, but my feet grounded in truth. So be it.

Winter

Winter's theme centers on taking a rest before rebirth occurs. In Wiccan traditions, this is a season for purification, introspection, and banishing any ghosts that linger in the closet. Through prayer, let the Divine cleanse any negativity, anxiety, or past wounds that hold you back spiritually.

As the sun's power seems all but gone, our minds also turn to those who have passed on to Summerland. Winter is a fitting season to pray for the peace of those souls. And for our own souls, ask for health, well-being, and the vision to keep hope in our hearts until spring comes again.

A winter prayer: *Ancient Ones, bend down your ears to hear my prayer. The world is quiet and resting. So too bring peace to my soul, and to the spirit(s) of* _____, [insert any names of people who have passed over] *who await reincarnation. Take any restlessness, any worry, and cover it in a healing blanket of snow.*

During this time of darkness, let me recognize my own shadows, but not be overcome by them. Let me also see that the night is not only full of shadows, but full of beauty and potential. The loveliness of stars, the wonders of my dreams. Hold me in your arms as I rest and sleep now, keeping hope in my heart until spring brings the dawn. Amen.

Thematic Prayers

> The deepest wishes of thy heart find expression in secret prayer.
>
> —George E. Rees

As we go through the ritual of life, inevitably we come to junctures when we seek out Divine help. All too often this happens when we've reached exasperation or total frustration and feel there's no other avenue through which to find assistance. I call this the "oh, God" syndrome. "Oh, God why...," "oh my God," and other similar phrases indicate that, consciously or subconsciously, humans are already aware of their need for the God/dess and of this Being's magical power. The problem is that we don't always act on that awareness in day-to-day life, even after a crisis.

By using prayer to prepare ourselves for living in the new millennium, we can change acts of desperation into moments of empowerment. How? Praying regularly means that we will already be in communion with the Source *before* emergencies arise, hopefully avoiding some of them altogether. Even when difficult situations do occur, the ritual of prayer teaches us how to communicate effectively with the Source for powerful, positive results.

Banishing

Nearly all religious traditions characterize the power of God as a brilliant light that can overcome any darkness. Banishing prayers, therefore, are focused on driving away evil or negative influences in our lives using that light as a force. These prayers also acknowledge that the self plays an intimate role in chasing shadows. One must have a real desire and willingness to change things or change cannot happen.

A banishing prayer: *Light of Light, blazing through all time, space, and dimensions, come! Illuminate the darkness that seems to engulf me. Push back the night until it becomes day once more. Don't allow the waves of* _____ [fill in with words for what you've been feeling, like *frustration, despair,* or *fear*] *to overwhelm me. Become my buoy, my strength through this storm.*

I am willing to fight—to stand up for truth and love. My resolve is strengthened knowing You're at my side. Help me to see clearly, to speak honestly, to hear and really listen, and to reach out for support when my determination waivers. Light of Light, hear this prayer, cast out the shadows wherever they may lie, including my own heart. So be it.

Fertility

Fertility is a double blessing. One type brings increased creativity, abundant friends or ideas, and other forms of fruitfulness. The second is more literal in nature, pertaining specifically to physical fertility. In both cases, prayer acts like water on the hopeful loam of your heart. And the God/dess is a terrific gardener.

Because the two focuses here are very distinct, I've provided samples for both.

A prayer for fruitfulness: *Gaia's Gardener, Originator of all that flourishes, see the desire of my heart. Grant your blessings on* _____ [describe briefly the project or area in your life that's the focus for the prayer]. *Let my efforts be like a seed: Blown by a gentle wind, rooted in rich soil, warmed by your light, and kept pure and nourished by spiritual rain.*

I know that the path ahead requires work and constancy to achieve my goal(s). Help to make that road less bumpy, give me the strength, _____ [fill in any other attributes you feel you'll need to experience the fruitfulness desired] *with which to persist, and light the way to success. Amen.*

A prayer for physical fertility: *Mother and Father of all creation, see the desire of my heart to be a parent. I do not make this request lightly and recognize that caring for another soul is a heavy responsibility. Yet, I welcome that task and ask that I might learn and grow as much as, if not more than, the child who comes into my life.*

I have made the space and time in my life and heart for a young spirit whom I wish to welcome to this earth plane. Prepare now my body for this sacred task. Allow the love between me and _____ [your partner's name] *to ignite the spark of life within, when the time is right. So be it.*

People who plan on adopting can use a similar prayer, changing the second section to ask for blessings on the legal process involved and the emotional support to endure that process with joyful anticipation.

Focus

Some situations naturally drive us to distraction. Nonetheless there are times when we really need to focus on one goal or circumstance instead of wasting energy on numerous, unproductive projects. When this occurs, our prayers reach out to the Source to get things back on track.

A prayer for focus: *Nucleus of the Universe, I have lost my way. My thoughts are scattered, my actions uncertain, my heart doubtful. Numerous _____ [choices, ideas, responsibilities, and so on] leave me hesitant to move, yet afraid to wait. Help me to find my focus again, to reclaim order in my life and mind. Help me listen to the still small voice within that knows what priority to set, and how to accomplish that goal. Give me a signpost to follow, from within or without, and set my eyes firmly upon it until the task is done. So be it.*

Health

I remember my mother always saying "If you have your health, you have everything." As a child, I didn't appreciate the wisdom of her words. As an adult, I have begun to understand them more intimately. When the body and mind get out of sync, it becomes nearly impossible to focus on spiritual pursuits. So in praying for health, the entire trinity that is our being should be mentioned.

A prayer for health: *Ancient Ones, I come before you to ask for renewal. Renew my body—give it strength, energy, and stamina with which to continue caring for myself* [and, if applicable, *my family*]. *Wherever sickness dwells, replace it with health. Renew my mind—give it peace, understanding, insight, and keen awareness so that faith has foundations in truth and reality. Wherever unhealthy thoughts dwell, replace them with hope.*

Renew my spirit—give it discernment, harmony, and the spark of all magic. Wherever darkness dwells, replace it with light. Let this shine from within to act as a beacon for all my actions and thoughts. So be it.

Happiness

Second to health, happiness is one of the prime ingredients that makes human life bearable, even when minor aggravations arise. But the question arises—what will make us truly happy? Joy is something that, while influenced by external situations, must truly be born within. So, prayers for happiness focus on generating the seed of joy in our hearts.

A prayer for happiness: *Lord of Song, Lady of Dance, see the heaviness of my heart—the waves of sadness that threaten to drown the spark of my spirit. Help me find the light of hope in this darkness and follow it back to wholeness.*

Let me find joy in the knowledge that I am not alone. Let me find happiness in myself, my gifts, my friends, and family. Remind me that the greatest blessings are not always part of the tangible world, but those that come in silent moments of the soul. Refill the well of my spirit now, till it overflows with gladness. So be it.

Jobs

An effective spiritual life has strong foundations in the material world. Work is the part of that reality that supports ourselves and our families. When one's job is frustrating, unsatisfying, inadequate to meet the budget, or when one is facing downsizing, it creates internal disharmony that influences every part of our reality. So our prayers for a positive work environment are not "selfish"— instead they ask to meet a verifiable need.

A prayer for work: *Great Provider, see my needs. I work at* _____ [fill in your company's name], *but lately that position has been difficult. The pressures of* _____ [bills, a performance review, layoffs, unappreciated efforts, or whatever] *surround me. Help me to do my best, despite the circumstances. Open the doors necessary to improve things and help me recognize those opportunities when they come. I am willing to walk whatever path you guide me down for personal and professional advancement. So be it.*

Love

The love of friends, family, or a significant other makes difficult situations easier to bear, and good circumstances all the more uplifting. When we pray for love in our lives, we should not forget the empowerment that can be found in loving ourselves more.

These prayers also seek to improve the quality of love we experience, and our ability to give and receive this valuable emotion.

A prayer for love: *Venus, Frigg, Cupid, Krishna, all the Powers who embody the spirit of love, I come to you. Fill every corner of my life with the wonder and power of love. Let me first love myself so that I appreciate the temple that houses my soul and all its amazing abilities. Help me to better accept love into my life by taking down any walls between me and those I care about.*

Today and every day let me show more love to others. Let my words be filled with kindness and truth. Let my thoughts be filled with good will. Let my heart overflow with charity and my actions reflect that energy. When I meet another in pain, let the love in and around my life act as a salve to his or her wounds. Help me to love freely and purely, without any expectations or selfishness as I walk the Path of Beauty. So be it.

Money

An old musical included a song with lyrics that said, "Money makes the world go round." This doesn't represent an overly romantic view of life, but in today's materialistic society, it's all too often true. Our spiritual pursuits don't mean much if we can't put food on the table and keep a roof over our heads. The goal of a money prayer, therefore, is to help us meet financial needs so we have the time and mental attitude with which to focus on spiritual ones.

A money prayer: *Ganesha, Dagda, Zeus, Freyr, Raphael, ye Lords of prosperity, hear my plea. My pockets are growing empty and my heart is full of worry. Help me find ways to improve the flow of money in my life so that bills get paid adequately and regularly. I recognize that I may have to give more of myself at a job to accomplish this task. Let me see such opportunities, and use them effectively.*

Lords of providence, see the truth of my neediness. Extend the vaults of heaven generously so I can care for _____ [note specific needs, like your family]. *When your blessings do come, help me to use them with wisdom and prudence. So be it.*

Passion

Passion is not something that just pertains to our sex lives. One can be passionate about a job, a cause, or beliefs. Passion is essentially a fervor that keeps a fire going under important relationships or situations, both mundane and spiritual. With the apathy bug biting so many people these days, a goodly dose of passion may be just what the world needs in the new millennium. Our prayers for passion reflect this need.

A prayer for passion: *Aphrodite, great goddess of passion, I feel nothing for those things that should have great meaning. My spirit is numb. May your abundant fire rekindle coals that have grown so very cold within me. Let me feel your energy building with each beat of my heart and every breath I take. Then release this power without to manifest in* _____ [fill in with the specific area in which you wish more passion].

Aphrodite, I would not ask such a boon without cause. You can see into my heart, see the dark clouds that linger there strangling the warmth. Banish that darkness, let me breathe and think and feel the fullness of passion once more. So be it.

Pets

For many people pets are like children to love and protect with equal diligence. In Wiccan tradition the whole of the animal kingdom is worthy of care and respect, so pets are valued. Some pets also become familiars—spiritual companions. Familiar or not, however, prayers for a pet simply invoke Divine blessings and health for that animal.

A prayer for pets: *Cerridwen, Faunus, hear my words and look upon* _____ [name of pet], *my pet and constant companion. He (or she) is part of the great network of life. I honor that network now by asking for your blessings on him (her). This* _____ [type of animal] *is more than just a toy, he (she) is a special addition to my family that I promise to care for and cherish. May your powers likewise watch over* _____, *keeping him (or her) happy and healthy until it is time to return to the earth. So be it.*

Protection

In world religious traditions one common theme is that of the Divine taking care of worshipers. This means protecting people from all manner of evil and negativity. With our world brimming with crime, war, pollution, greed, and other deadly sins, this protection becomes all the more important to living positively in the new millennium. Consequently, our prayers for protection can take on a similar universal, all-purpose theme.

A protection prayer: *Light of purity, protection, and power, shine on me, my home, and every place I go. Seek out every point of malevolence and negativity and chase it away from me. Lead me not along paths where such evil lies. Shine only on the Path of Spirit and walk with me along that road.*

All around me the darkness lingers—wishing to steal hope—but it cannot prevail. The tree of my spirit is grounded in truth and grows toward you. As I turn my hands skyward, help me catch your light within them and put it in my heart where none can take it away. Glory of Creation, hear this prayer. Let your light pour over me like a fountain, washing away any evil, and granting safe harbor wherever I may be. So be it.

Providence

Providence does not necessarily mean abundance or wealth. Instead, it speaks of daily maintenance—keeping food on the table, providing shelter, and the like. Taking a cue from the Psalms, the Universe can meet these basic needs, and thereby generate peace of mind and soul.

A prayer for providence: *Great Spirit, who resides in all things, I come before you in a time of need. I find my body, mind, spirit, and pocket lacking in the sustenance necessary to healthy, fulfilled living. Look throughout the network of creation for an answer to this need and help me to recognize that answer when it comes.*

Until then, grant me patience and trust. Energize my body with hopefulness so I can continue mundane efforts to bring about change. Engender peace in my restless mind and power in my drained spirit. With faith and thankfulness I ask it. So be it.

Strength and Courage

Our lives today may seem simpler in many ways than that of our ancestors, yet many circumstances still "try men's [and women's] souls." I suspect there will be many such days ahead in the new millennium, as it will be a time when our communal spirits get refined. So, when you find yourself facing a proverbial trial by fire, pray for fortitude, bravery, and endurance.

A prayer for strength and courage: *Hercules, great hero, uplift my weary spirit with your strength and vigor. I am facing my own twelve labors—to overcome anger, hatred, greed, prejudice, short-sightedness, frustration, unrealistic temptations, bad habits, outmoded thoughts, apathy, pessimism, and injustice* [note: Substitute other things in your life that are particularly pressing and vexing]. *I know the path of spirit is long and narrow. Keep my feet sure, my eyes keen, and my resolve steadfast. Take my hand in yours and lead the way to achievement, first within my own heart and soul, then in the world. So be it.*

Victory and Success

There are moments when we feel like the important things in our lives have come to a standstill. If any progress is being made, we just can't see it. Overcoming this delay requires patience and an understanding of exactly why blockage exists. Prayer can help provide that insight and begin the forward motion necessary for attainment.

A prayer for victory and success: *Kwan Yin, Goddess of mercy, she who is said to answer all sincere prayers, I call to you. I stand at an impass. I know not the way; no matter what I try, the obstacles remain firm.*

What lesson does this wall teach me? What benefit is there in waiting? Why can I not move ahead? These are the questions that lay heavy on my heart. If I am to move, guide my way. If I am to tarry, help me stay. Grant me your vision but for a moment so I can think and act wisely for the best possible outcome. So be it.

Prayers for Children

The simple heart that freely asks in love, obtains.

—John Greenleaf Whittier

There was a time that one of the first rhymes a child learned was a prayer to keep himself safe while asleep. Now the first thing children learn is how to use the remote control. As with other aspects of our society, this change reflects negatively on the human spiritual condition. The nucleus of our lives has become technology instead of Spirit.

Our children embody what the future will bring, which means we should teach them in the "way they should grow." Some Wiccans hesitate to educate their children in the Craft because of the difficulties this religion still faces in the mainstream. Nonetheless, I believe we can give our children ways and words that help them focus on being good people and the spiritual nature of all things, without those lessons implying anything about witchcraft. Prayer is one of those gifts.

Children's prayers need to have simple words and ideas, and they need to grow with that child. Those given here are for younger children and should be modified to reflect a child's mental understanding as needed.

Family and Friends

Children want to see their family and friends be happy, which is why so many children's prayers include phrases like "bless Mommy, and Daddy, and. . . ." This is a child's simple way of expressing her love toward the people close to her. This unadorned love and honesty of intention is also why children's prayers are so powerful.

A prayer for family and friends: *Great Mother and Father, take care of my parents and the people I love. I'm little and feel like I can't help them as much as I want, so I'm asking for you to help. Keep*

_____ [fill in with names] *happy and healthy, and give them more time to spend with me so we can be a strong family.*

Thank you for giving me such good friends. They make me laugh when I'm sad or sick. Help me to see when they need help, too, and help me to give it without having to be asked. Sometimes I forget. Take care of _____ [fill in with friend's names] *wherever they may be. Thank you for this and all your goodness.*

Forgiveness

Children usually want to please people and when they do something "bad," it's hard for them to forgive themselves. Similarly, when other people are mean to a child, it's hard for him to quickly forgive that failing. This prayer is intended to begin the healing process within and without.

A prayer for forgiveness: *Mother and Father of all things, I'm sorry. It's hard to do the right thing all the time. I start thinking about what I want and forget what my parents told me. I feel really bad for hurting their feelings. Help them forgive me and help me be a better son (daughter). When I go to do something wrong, help me hear the little voice in my heart that knows better. Make that voice shout so it muffles whatever's tempting me. Thank you for your help and for making me feel better. So be it.*

Harmony

One of the most distressing situations to a child is when people in her home fight or carry a lot of tension. The child often feels as if she is somehow responsible. This prayer gives the child a chance to do something positive about the problem, without having to openly discuss her anxieties with anyone but the Divine.

A prayer for harmony: *Spirit of Peace, I'm very sad today.* _____ *and* _____ [fill in appropriately] *have been fighting. Everyone is saying really nasty things that I know they don't mean. Everyone is mad and not really listening. I don't know what to do and I need your help. Reach out, touch us, and calm everyone down so we can talk and work things out. Bring peace back to my home and family. So be it.*

Health

When a child, or someone he loves, becomes ill, he may feel there's nothing he can do to help. The adults are the ones who administer medicines, take temperatures, and so forth. But no one can tell a child that he is not old enough to pray for health. Prayer gives a child a sense of control and something positive to contribute.

A prayer for health: *Spirit of Health, hear my prayer. _____ [fill in with the person's name] is sick. He (she) feels really bad. I can send my good wishes, but you can make him (her) feel better. Give _____ more energy, more hope, and help them rest so him (her) can do all the things he (she) likes to do. Send _____ a hug from me, and hold him (her) tight until he (she) is well. Thank you.*

Peer Pressure

As children get older, one of the greatest issues becomes whom to listen to—parents or peers. Many of the trials and temptations facing our youth are physically dangerous, meaning they need to develop the inner fortitude to stand up for what's right. Prayer is one way of strengthening that resolve.

A prayer for handling peer pressure: *Spirit of Strength, help me now. The people around me want me to do things that aren't right. They taunt and tease me because I say no, and saying no is getting harder and harder. Please stand by me and hold my hand so I can feel you. Let my words be loud and strong when I know that I'm doing the right thing. Let those kids hear what I'm saying and leave me alone. As long as you stay with me I'm never alone. So be it.*

Pleasant Dreams

Every child experiences the occasional nightmare. When she wakes up, fear and anxiety overwhelm the knowledge that "It was only a dream." In these moments a prayer becomes one way of allaying that fear through faith. Also, depending on the wording of the prayer, it can help a child learn to take control of her dreams.

A prayer for pleasant dreams: *Sandman, Seer of Dreams, stop these pictures that frighten me so. The dreams close in on me until I can't think, can't breathe, and I feel like everything's against me. I get so scared I can't run or hide or go back to sleep.*

As I put my head on my pillow, take away the fear; take away those pictures in my mind. Let me imagine pretty trees, a stream, some birds, and a bright sunny sky. Let me see kites flying, my favorite pet playing with me, my family watching over us [parents: Offer suitable substitutes in visualization here]. *And when I do go to sleep again, please catch and carry away any bits of sand that have nightmares in them, so I don't have to be afraid anymore. So be it.*

Prayers for Earth Healing

Converse with God through nature.

—G. B. Cheevery

In Wicca and many other spiritual traditions, the earth is regarded as far more than just an amalgam of rock and water. The earth is a reflection of, and dwelling place for, the Great Spirit. It is also a living, breathing organism worthy of respect.

Humans are slowly becoming more aware of their intimate responsibility to this organism. We have a lot of cleanup work to do to repair the damage done in the name of progress. Long into the new millennium, the planet will need our dutiful care and attention to recuperate. These prayers are part of that caring process.

Earth Awareness

In order to become conscientious caretakers of this planet, we must first make ourselves more aware of it. This includes nature's cycles, signs, and spiritual lessons. While we walk on sacred ground each day, few of us even notice a passing ant, a new sprig of grass, or a bird overhead. The purpose of this prayer is to manifest a renewed awareness and appreciation for all corners of creation.

A prayer for earth awareness: *Earth Goddess, by all your great names—Gaia, Demeter, Inanna, Isis, hear my prayer. Help me and the citizens of Earth to remain ever attentive to this planet and how our actions affect it. Help us to better appreciate the beauty of earth's seasons, the wonder of flowers and fruit, the glory of animals in their natural environment, the warmth of grass beneath our feet.*

As I go about my daily tasks, harmonize my spirit with your cycles, attune my soul to your voice, synchronize my heart to your rhythm. Let me approach each day as a miracle and an opportunity to serve you. So be it.

Gaia's Body

Earth's body is composed of molten lava, soil and rock, plants, trees, animals, atmosphere, and weather. Each part of this ecosystem has strong correlations with our own bodies—blood, skin, arms, legs, breath, and emotions, respectively. As animistic as this metaphor seems, without an understanding of earth's body and how it works, we cannot hope to heal it. This prayer encourages that understanding and asks for the healing process to begin with us.

A prayer for the planet: *Creator, look upon this beautiful blue world and see its wounds. I and others have left scrapes, scars, and open sores across the land, sea, and skies. We cannot roll back the pages of time and make the ugliness go away, but we can learn from our mistakes. Help that process to begin in my heart today, and every day.*

Teach me to hear the words of the wind, the whispers of waves, the music of sunlight, the dancing of rain, and all the other voices of the elements as they join in the chorus of life. Teach me to honor those voices, and those of all earth's creatures, and treasure them with reverence. Give me the strength, vision, and wisdom I need to become a good caretaker for the sacred space of Earth. So be it.

Gaia's Mind

Earth's mind is her intelligent inhabitants (namely us). This collective mind needs many things to serve the earth better: oneness, accord, thoughtfulness, and wisdom to name a few. So, our prayers for Gaia's mind reflect the things it lacks, or that sorely need improvement.

A prayer for Gaia's mind: *Janus, God who sees both past and future, look upon this world with merciful eyes. The mind of Gaia has grown ill with all manner of dis-ease, yet you have the vision and wisdom to help us. Let us peer from your perspective for but a moment, to know what might have been...what could still be if we change the way we live. Help us to learn that reciprocity with Nature takes thoughtfulness—day to day, moment to moment, making each one count.*

For myself as part of this collective mind, I ask for awareness and respect, even for the smallest things. Let me walk gently on this world so beauty replaces destruction; so that life replaces death. Let me leave behind a world that is better for my time upon it. So be it.

Gaia's Spirit

The spirit of Earth has been called by many names, Gaia being but one of them. No matter the culture or historical setting, this spirit symbolizes the vibrant abundance of the planet—its plants, animals, and the network of life. Wiccans continue to see it as such and pray for its continued well-being.

A prayer for Gaia's spirit: *Lord and Lady whose power created the Big Bang, whose essence gave life and soul to this world, hear my prayer. The spirit of Gaia is weakened and weeping. It weeps for her children who know not what they do. It weeps for the raping of her mountains and meadows, and the creatures who will never return home.*

Find the salve to ease this sadness and rejuvenate her spirit. And, once found, let my hands be those that help to apply it. Embrace the planet with warm, white light, like a hug to chase the shadows of darkness. Embrace Gaia in your protective care until we can make her whole once more. So be it.

Prayers for the New Millennium

The greatest prayer is patience.

— Buddha

The future, in many ways, is both already here and always arriving. It is part of our thoughts and will be influenced by all our past and present actions. This knowledge can sometimes seem overwhelming in terms of personal and planetary responsibility. But, instead of worrying about tomorrow, we can live beneficially today, using the energy of prayer to guide our way. Prayer is one way to welcome and live in the new era using positive spiritual power as an ally.

Forgiveness

We cannot hope to achieve a better future without first forgiving the past. As much as we might wish otherwise, there are times when we hurt people, times when we stumble on our spiritual path, and times when we make serious mistakes. Prayer opens the way for healing between two or more people, between the self and the Universe, and perhaps most importantly, within our own hearts.

Forgiveness prayer: *Pax, the essence of peace, settle once more in my heart and soul. Much has happened for which I am not proud. I've fallen along the Path of Beauty, and find it hard to stand once more. It's as if the wind of Spirit has been knocked out of me and the light eludes me. Please, reach down with a helping hand and help me find my way home.*

Let me integrate the important lessons of this experience so history doesn't repeat itself. Let me remain conscious of what has happened so I can repair the damage done to myself or anyone else. But don't let me dwell in self pity or condemnation—those feelings bear no life, no wellbeing, and serve nothing positive. Replace them with the hope that comes from a new awareness, change, and a readiness to meet the future as a better person for my experiences. So be it.

Improved Communications

One of the things that keeps people apart is their inability to communicate effectively with one another. Communication is a two-way street—that means that for our communications to change, all people have to learn how to speak sensitively, listen intuitively, and respond prudently. The prayer for communication includes all these factors.

A prayer for improved communication: *Hermes, messenger of the Gods, hear my prayer. Braggi, divine guardian of the nectars of the muses, hear my prayer. While the people of earth speak many languages, we all have similar desires and dreams. Help us share these with one another in gentleness and truth.*

No matter the tongue or setting, help us find a universal language with which to know each other—not by color, culture, or creed, but as fellow human beings. Even when we differ in opinions, let our words be sweet upon our lips, kind, insightful, and filled with peaceful intentions. Let our conversations be honest, built on a foundation of mutual respect, nurtured by mutual aspiration, to eventually blossom with love. So be it.

Religious Tolerance

There is something in human nature that yearns to win an argument. With religion, the arguments are emotional and deep because we're speaking of the unprovable and intangible. Be that as it may, to truly bless the new millennium with our magic, that magic has to become more accepted and respected. Religious tolerance encourages a nurturing atmosphere for all faiths.

Wiccans feel that all paths to the Divine have equal merit for, and benefit to, those who walk them. The most important thing is taking the first step; so prayers for religious tolerance work toward that first, teetering, baby-step forward, in understanding each other.

A prayer for religious tolerance: *God/dess, your names and faces are many. Your ideals have been tinted by cultures, eras, politics, and social trends. Yet, the core of Universal Truth remains—in every tree and brook, every star and stone. This is the nucleus of all humankind's spirits. Help us to see this central root as a binding tie through which we can all be nurtured.*

While our words are different, they mean much the same. The differences that separate us come from limited human vision, which cannot look beyond dogma. Broaden our understanding and vision to see as you see, to identify each other as brothers and sisters of Spirit.

The path of beauty is many things to many people, but it always leads back to you. Help us recognize that you are the Sacred Parent. Any Power so great as to create our diversity cannot be confined to one image or one creed. Help us find wonder and joy in our differences and appreciate our similarities. Today and always we are all children of one family, both Divine yet mortal—the family of man. Let acceptance among people of all faiths be cherished as a great virtue. So be it.

World Peace

As we go through our day-to-day routine, it's easy to forget that we are not *just* part of a family, town, or city. We are citizens of earth and need to think and act globally to encourage a peaceful future. It is one thing to know this truth, and another altogether to live it.

To achieve world peace, we must all give 110 percent, including in our prayers. The time for Divine intervention and miracles is not past. Let's make a new millennium in which all of humankind's evils are replaced with peace and understanding. It can begin with a quiet, diligent soul in prayer.

A prayer for world peace: *Guardian of all that is Sacred, our world is hurting. People are hurting. War, crime, apathy, and negativity threaten to destroy the wonders of earth and its inhabitants. Reach out from the center of the Universe and motivate the winds of change. Help save us from ourselves.*

Today, if you will guide me, I vow my hands, heart, and magic to the goal of world peace. Let me be gentle with myself and others. Let me care for those around me, no matter our differences. Where anger dwells, help

me bring harmony; where I see apathy, help me inspire; where there is neg-
ativity, help me affirm and uplift.

Before the waves of conflict swell beyond the walls of goodness and
decency, help all humankind do likewise. Let the walls that separate us
come tumbling down, dismantled by honest effort and random acts of kind-
ness. Drop a blanket of peace upon this planet, to wrap us all in whole-
ness once more. For our children, and our children's children, let it be so.

When all is said and done, and the Universe answers your needs,
please remember to say "thank you"—even when a prayer is not
answered exactly as you hoped. A grateful heart is one filled with
joy and appreciation for what it has, instead of forever chasing
what it has not. It is also one that will see the beauty and wonder
of the Universe at work, even subtly, because it is ready to give
and receive.

3

Meditation and Visualization

Meditation is the eye wherewith we see God.

—St. Ambrose, A.D. 340

Almost all spiritual disciplines set aside time for some type of quiet reflection and meditation. Exactly what this time accomplishes depends much on the tradition and setting. A physician, for example, might recommend soothing meditations as a tool for decreasing high blood pressure or pain. For some New Age practitioners, meditation integrates and "marries" ideas and beliefs with one's spirit so they can manifest in action. In religious settings, meditation prepares one's mind and spirit for communing with the Divine before a ritual.

Practitioners of Transcendental Meditation use it as a relaxation technique that inspires inner-connectedness and focus. Taoists employ meditation to banish unwanted thoughts and search for stillness within. Masonic traditions see meditation as an aid to understanding ancient mysteries and clarifying our vision of the universe. Without this understanding and clarity, they predict that civilization will continue in a state of spiritual uncertainty—an interesting observation as we move into, and live in, a new millennium.

Summing up these diverse ideas: Since divination provides us with insight, and prayer provides attitude, meditation then provides a new or refreshed spiritual awareness. This awareness naturally changes our outlook and the way we behave. Johnathan Edwards, an American theologian of the 1700s, expressed this when he said, "ideas and images in our minds govern action." Goethe, a German philosopher living during the same era, felt similarly saying, "to make them truly yours [wise thoughts] we must think them over again honestly, till they take root in our personal experience."

Wiccans agree that meditation helps generate positive actions toward change and improvement. Generally speaking, Wiccans use meditation to cast off the tensions, negativity, and behaviors of the mundane world, and make themselves a sacred space within which a positive attitude and intention dwell. Once this mental space is established, we can contemplate our spiritual path, consider alternative outlooks, assimilate new information, integrate beneficial virtues, empower our spells or rituals, or simply enjoy a moment's peace.

The importance of this last point shouldn't be underestimated. Humankind's spirit has shown signs of being very restless in recent history, probably due to neglect. Stopping for a moment to breathe, gear down, and remember your place in the universe will naturally help generate inner peace. Once you achieve peace within, its much easier to manifest it without. I truly believe that daily meditation can become an important, enjoyed exercise. Consider it like taking a daily spiritual vitamin that makes for a healthy soul, improved resistance to negativity, and increased energy on all levels of your being.

Effective Meditation

There is no life of the spirit without the imagination.

—Ann Ulanov

The dictionary defines meditation as continued thought—the serious contemplation, turning, or revolving of a subject in the mind, often of a religious nature. This means, knowingly or not, that everyone meditates to some degree every day. Each time you ponder a decision, an idea presented, a perplexing situation or question, or the like, you are meditating. The main difference between this daily form of thoughtfulness and esoteric meditation is regimen and methodology.

SEVEN STEPS TO EFFECTIVE MEDITATION

1. Insure yourself of quiet, uninterrupted time.
2. Find a comfortable place where you can sit without fidgeting. Try the traditional cross-legged posture.
3. Breathe deeply and evenly, so that each breath becomes a connected circle with nearly unnoticeable seams between the inhale and the exhale.
4. Release your tensions and everyday thoughts.
5. Develop the visualization in as much detail as possible.
6. Add any verbalizations that support the goal of the visualization.
7. Slowly increase the amount of time you spend in meditation, and be patient with yourself.

No matter the religious path, effective meditation methods bear similarities to one another. For example, it's common for people to sit cross-legged as they meditate. This creates an upright triangle, formed by points of both knees and the head, the traditional seat of the Divine. In esoteric traditions, an upright triangle represents the element of fire whose flame symbolizes the immutable human spirit. So, this traditional posture accents the spiritual goals of meditation and helps keep the meditator awake. The deeply relaxed state induced by meditation makes sleep very tempting, and, as Buddha said, "Everything comes down to one thing: staying awake!"

Second, meditating in a peaceful location also seems common and has a very important purpose. The human mind is accustomed to thinking about numerous things at once. External noise or activity only increases potential distractions. Finding a quiet place gives the meditator a better chance of successfully retraining his mind to concentrate on one, and only one, thing—the purpose of the meditation. Mind you, most people new to meditation find other distractions anyway—their nose will itch, their leg may fall asleep, and so forth. This is perfectly normal so be patient with yourself. Meditation is a *discipline*, meaning, it takes time and diligence to develop.

I can already hear complaints from readers who say they have no personal space, and even less time to develop such a discipline. My suggestion to these people is to try the bathroom. It sounds silly, but it's one of the few places you can be ensured privacy, and where you have to sit down for a few minutes anyway! You won't achieve an overly deep level of meditation during these attempts, but the practice will help improve your efforts when time and circumstances allow for longer sittings.

Three other components seem somewhat universal to effective meditation methods: metered breathing, visualization, and verbalization. Breathing slowly and evenly encourages relaxation and centeredness. It also naturally revitalizes our reserves by bearing life-giving oxygen to every cell in our body. A good breathing technique to try is taking in a deep breath on the count of three, holding it for a count of three, and releasing it on the count of three. Repeat this pattern until it becomes all-connected and you don't have to consciously think about it (see also Pre-meditation Groundwork later in this chapter).

Visualization allows us to review the meditation's focus or goal from a detached, enhanced perspective. For all intents and purposes, visualization is nothing more than directed, purposeful imagining. Adults tend to discount the power of a will-powered imagination, but this is the same font from which our creativity, resourcefulness, and inspiration flow. The power to make and change our minds dwells within, and visualization is one tool that unlocks that power.

Visualizations vary depending on the need. For example, a person trying to clear out negativity might visualize dark light being expelled from her body, and white light being absorbed. An individual wishing to overcome an obstacle in his life might imagine himself tearing down a wall. The nice part about a visualization is that you can personalize and change the symbols to suit any situation, goal, or need—be it spiritual or mundane. In fact, the more you individualize a visualization, the greater your chance of success. Why? Because you used emblems that have deep personal meaning, and the mind has a lot of talent for which we rarely give it due credit.

Verbalization adds a second, sensual dimension to the visualization's inner-imagery: hearing. When used correctly, verbalizations result in a wave of energy. This energy mirrors and supports our meditative goal(s). In more contemporary terms, the sound produces "good vibes" that saturate the meditation space and the person meditating.

Exactly what form the verbalization takes depends on one's personal preference and spiritual path. One option is chanting. Chants are monophonic words and phrases with a songlike quality, which bear some similarity to incantations. A common chant in Wiccan circles is one that represents and energizes the four elements within the speaker. I'm sorry to say I don't know who originated this, but it's an excellent example:

> *Air I am*
> *Fire I am*
> *Water, Earth, and Spirit I am*

A second option is using a mantra—rhythmic sacred words or verses, which can also act as prayer. In Hindu tradition specifically, the word *mantra* means "lore" or "learning." It is a kind of password that helps an individual elevate herself to a higher spiritual awareness. *Om*, or *Om mani padme Hum* is a familiar example. *Om* represents the self, the Universe, and the unity that can be achieved between the two.

A third option that appeals to those seeking more user-friendly phrases are affirmations. Affirmations are simple, positive, uplifting expressions. For example, a person whose meditative goal is improved well-being might repeat the phrase, "I am whole," as he visualizes and concentrates on that goal.

Creating Your Own Meditations and Visualizations

In a book of this nature it would be nearly impossible to detail exercises to which everyone could relate, and which could serve every human need. In instances where you want to adapt a given meditation, or create your own, keep the following information in mind. A good meditation

- contains a core—a main theme or goal around which the entire meditation revolves. This core remains consistent throughout the meditation. For example, in the seasonal meditations that follow, a tree is used to represent the self. The type of tree does not change in the middle of the meditation, nor does a bird suddenly replace the tree as the central emblem.
- includes people, places, and things with which you are familiar, and ones that relate to the meditation's theme or goal. For example, in a meditation for peace, a person who has never been to the mountains might find that setting difficult to visualize, no matter how calm it may sound. So, she might substitute another quiet retreat (perhaps a forest) that she can imagine fully.
- contains symbols that emphasize that theme you personally relate to. For example, it would be hard for someone with a fear of water to effectively utilize a healing water visualization. This person would have to find another symbol, like a bandage, that he associates with feeling better.
- follows a sequence that creates a successful outcome or emphasizes positive, life-affirming energy. For example, someone tack-

ling a difficult illness might visualize himself battling that sickness in a boxing ring and winning by a knock out toward the end of the meditation. This symbolism emphasizes the desire to "knock out" the malady

In deciding exactly what to meditate about, and what other elements the meditation should include, just look to your life for guidance. If you want to improve your communication skills, for example, you might meditate on the way you usually speak and add a verbalization to transform and energize that speech. A visualization could be added, too—perhaps the image of your mouth expelling brilliant, smooth, white light that forms words.

It may take a little time to find just the right combination of elements that makes the meditation feel right, but the time will be well spent. This process compels you to think about the core issue in detail, which is a type of meditation in and of itself. By the time you finish creating the meditation you're really mentally and spiritually prepared to use it effectively!

Nine Helpful Hints

1. For those of you who have trouble reading a meditation and remembering its content later, I suggest taping your exercises. Record them yourself or have a friend read them slowly for you. This way you can listen, step-by-step, and follow the imagery like you might a really good story on the radio. Actually, this is a good method for everyone to try at least once. You'll find it releases the pressure of memorization and allows you to concentrate wholly on the goal of the meditation. Most people feel this improves the results.

2. If you're in a situation that makes the verbal portion of a meditation uncomfortable, *think* the phrases instead. Thoughts are the initiating energy behind our words. They carry just as much power and the same vibrations as the words themselves. And, if you listen with your inner ears, you can still hear those thoughts as vividly as if they were spoken out loud.

3. It's not necessary to concentrate on just one meditation theme or goal at a time, but I wouldn't try doing more than three different ones concurrently. For one thing, few people have enough free time to allow for several meditation sittings in a day. If you decide to master more than one meditation, separate each exercise with a period of rest or diversion. This gives your mind a break and allows it to shift to a different focus more easily upon entering the new meditation.

Some other touches that improve harmonic sensual input and generally enhance the meditative state and the results include:

4. burning incense with an aroma that matches the theme or goal of the meditation.

5. meditating in a candlelit room, using the candle flame as a temporary focus before closing your eyes.

6. playing soft, instrumental music that somehow reflects the theme or goal of the meditation.

7. taking a warm bath or shower beforehand to accentuate relaxation. If you're tense, meditation is very difficult.

8. fasting, if physically feasible, for a short time before the meditation. Fasting cleanses the body and increases spiritual awareness.

9. meditating on a regular basis—if possible, for at least five minutes daily.

What to Expect

Faith is the touching of a mystery.

—Alexander Schmemann

The results of meditation vary from individual to individual. Much depends on a person remaining patient and persistent. The more committed you are, the better results your efforts will yield. Each time you meditate on a topic or goal, your mind slowly adjusts to the imagery provided. Consciously or subconsciously, it continues to mull over that imagery until eventually integration or attainment occurs. So, each time you meditate on the same topic again, you actually help accelerate the integration/attainment process by restressing the importance of this issue to your mind.

From a strictly physical viewpoint, meditation has been proven to decrease stress-related problems and improve the immune system. Even if these are the *only* positive effects you experience from meditation, I'd say it's well worth the effort. From a spiritual perspective, meditation brings us into closer union with Sacred energies. It generates a better understanding of life's network, liberates us from negative energies, draws in positive vibrations, guides the quest for enlightenment, and empowers our magic.

Such results, however, are the product of time and practice. Deep spiritual awareness isn't an award to be contended for solely to laud the accomplishment, so it's rarely instantaneous. We need to work honestly toward it so that, once achieved, the perception is honored and guarded as a true treasure.

For simple thematic matters, such as understanding a problem better, I suggest that you meditate over several days at least. Each time you review the situation, you should get more insight. Make notes of your experiences and read them over later.

More difficult things, such as dispelling lifelong attitudes and habits, aren't so quick to resolve. After all, they were *years* in the making. Expecting one or two meditation sittings to fix everything is just unrealistic. Dedicate yourself to several *months,* or even a *year,* of committed meditation on the subject. Again, I suggest making notes of your experiences. These will often reveal progress upon review, which then provides more confidence and hope to continue trying.

Pre-Meditation Groundwork

In the interest of not repeating the same procedure at the outset of each meditation in this chapter, take the following steps jsut prior to beginning these exercises.

1. Set up any desired incense, candles, music, etc.
2. Dim the lighting in the room (or draw curtains).
3. Shake out your arms and legs. Shrug and roll your shoulders and head to release tension.
4. Sit cross-legged, or if that's not possible, lie flat on a comfortable but firm surface.
5. Close your eyes and listen to the sounds of your heart and breath. Just stay still and listen for two to three minutes to get back in touch with your body's rhythm.
6. Begin breathing in through your nose and out through your mouth, slowly and evenly. Let the breath become all-connected so that it's hard to tell where one breath ends and another begins. Keep breathing this way for at least three minutes until you feel totally relaxed and mentally uncluttered.
7. Start the meditation.
8. At the end of the meditation, sit and take notes of the experience. Don't get up or move too quickly. This will disrupt the soothing effect of the meditation, resulting in dizziness or a headache.

Seasonal Meditations

Earth, teach me stillness…

—Ute Prayer

Seasonal meditations are somewhat unique in that they often achieve results after one try. Why? Because a seasonally focused meditation brings the individual into harmony with the earth's cycle, and the focal points of that cycle. Since humans are animals, they often have a subconscious, instinctual awareness of this already. The meditation simply activates that awareness, taking it out of idle and putting it into gear.

For the purpose of congruity, each of these meditations uses the imagery of a tree as a starting point. The tree represents the self: The roots are your feet, the trunk is your back, and the top represents your arms and head. In determining what type of tree you will be, choose one you can visualize clearly and the foliage of which changes with the season.

Spring

In your mind's eye, see yourself as you are right now, in as much detail as possible. Slowly allow the furniture around you to transform into small bushes, flowers, and other natural objects. Allow the room and ceiling to fade away, replaced by a forest canopy.

All around you plants are still touched with the slightest hint of snow and ice. Beneath this, new grass is pushing its way up toward the sun. Other than an occasional bird, the forest is hushed and very peaceful. Accept the calm as part of yourself...breathe it in like air.

As you sit among the plants, small tendrils appear in your feet and legs. They reach to the earth to embrace it and immediately turn into woody roots. You can feel the roots burrowing in the rich, cool soil, filled with moisture from the thaw. Your body becomes a tree trunk, secured to the ground by the roots. Your arms become naked branches, with nothing but buds to keep them warm in spring's chilly winds.

If you look, you'll notice the sun slowly rising on the horizon. Its warmth makes sap move more quickly through every part of the self-tree, energizing and awakening your senses. You can feel the earth and its creatures awakening with you. Linger in this moment of revival, sensing earth's breath in each breeze and knowing it as your own.

Stay as long as you wish, until you feel wholly refreshed and attuned to nature, then slowly adjust your breathing to a normal pace. See yourself transform back into a person. Open your eyes and make notes of the experience.

Summer

In your relaxed state, visualize the forest from the spring meditation, only this time the trees and plants are covered with leaves and flowers. The air is filled with the scent of roses and the sounds of happily buzzing insects. Listen to their song as it drones with earth's vibrations.

Below you the earth also pulsates with life. The water in the soil flows freely, taken up by your roots into the well of your spirit. Drink fully of this nourishing elixir until you feel you can drink no more.

Overhead the noonday sun shines brightly. Reach upward to greet these radiant beams, to embrace them, and welcome the sun god's energy into your spirit. Feel the cleansing power as the golden rays are absorbed by your leaves and branches. The warmth fills every cell in your body, chasing away any lingering sickness or negativity.

Remain in the sunlight; breathe deeply of it and the warm summer airs until you feel totally rejuvenated. Then, return to your normal self and breathing patterns, making notes of your experiences.

Fall

In your visualization, you walk into the forest at twilight. The trees all around you now bear leaves in red, orange, yellow, and a hint of brown. Sit near one of these trees, and slowly transform into your tree-self, the color in your leaves reflecting that of the neighboring foliage.

Once you've completely transformed, stop and assess how the earth around you feels. Everything is slowing down, settling, preparing to sleep. Consider ways that you, too, can slow down a little and simplify your life. Slow your breathing a little more and feel peace settle over you like a balm to your weary soul.

Feel the tree of self. Do you notice how the sap moves more slowly through you now? How your leaves feel like they're barely holding onto the branches? Let the leaves fall; they represent burdens in your life that you no longer need to bear. Release them to the earth, to the soil. Now your branches feel much lighter, much easier to sustain even without as much sunlight.

Enjoy the feeling of liberation and ease; relax in the cool fall air—let it refresh your spirit. Then, slowly return your visualization and breathing to the normal self and make notes of the experience.

Winter

The Sacred forest is hushed and calm when you come into it by night. The moon illuminates snowflakes gently falling to the ground. The trees are bare but for some icicles that hang off the branches like Nature's Yule decorations. Settle yourself into the snow and transform into a barren tree.

All around the earth is still. Birds are quiet. Animals are hibernating, and even the soil seems to be asleep beneath the white blanket. Now, as your branches reach to the sky, there is little warmth to greet them. Your sap moves very slowly.

The moon overhead is welcoming and comforting. You have all you can do to stay awake. The sense of restfulness is overwhelming. This is a moment of magic—a moment that hangs on the edge between winter and spring, just before the wheel turns again. But for now you will sleep in the Mother's loving arms. Tarry in restfulness as long as you need, then awaken renewed.

Thematic Meditations

> To grasp God in all things, this is the sign of your new birth.
>
> —Meister Eckhart

As with prayers, thematic meditations speak directly to pressing matters and human needs, be they physical, mental, or spiritual.

When a situation arises that motivates meditation, look for the core issue or need. This becomes the nucleus around which the meditation centers.

Before using any of the meditations in this section, review them to make sure you understand, and relate to, the central imagery. If not, try to substitute something else that you can see clearly, three-dimensionally, that makes more sense to you. To find the right imagery consider your personal experiences. For example, if your mother always knew how to make you feel better, perhaps she should administer the light of well-being in the healing meditation. This kind of personalization is very important. Without it, and without an emotional and spiritual connection to the images, meditation is an exercise in futility.

Banishing Negative Patterns

Humans are creatures of habit, not all of which are good for us. When you discover a negative pattern in your life, use this meditation to help change or eradicate it.

Begin your visualization in a classroom with a large blackboard. This is the classroom of life, and you are the only student present.

Walk up to the blackboard and write the negative pattern in your life upon it. Use symbols or words, whichever is easiest for you, then sit down in front of the board. Think about this pattern; when and why it occurs, and especially why it no longer should be part of you. Try to see the situation from various angles—how it affects you, those you love, your work. Direct the energy of the feelings that surface about this pattern toward the words or symbols on the blackboard in the form of a light beam. Pour any remnants of negativity, anger, frustration, and so forth into the lettering. When you feel empty, see yourself standing up, taking the eraser in hand, and literally erasing that pattern from your life. Turn your back on the board and walk out of the room. Don't look back—that chapter in your life is closed. Return to normal breathing and make notes of your experience. Repeat as needed.

Connecting With the Sacred

A small spark of the God/dess dwells within us all. The problem is recognizing and connecting with that energy. This meditation helps.

Visualize yourself walking down a long hallway filled with doors. Look at each door you pass. Some are square, some are round, some are triangular...when you find the one shaped like a heart, stop walking. Reach forward and try the handle. The door is locked, but you have the key you need in your pocket. Take it out, unlock the door, and enter.

Inside, a sacred temple awaits. The decorations and symbols are all very familiar to you. The minute you cross the threshold, you feel the ancient powers vibrating in the stone, wood, and glass. It takes your breath away, but it isn't frightening. To the contrary, you sense a presence bidding you to come in further. It's like a magnet drawing you ever closer to the source of Power.

You arrive in front of a dais. Above, you see a figure—neither male nor female, yet both—standing with hands stretched forward. The presence is incredible, beautiful, expansive, and magical. Move forward and take the figure's hands in your own. As you do, two hands become one and begin to blossom in a rosebud. The energy in your body swells to a crescendo as the rosebud opens fully, releasing its aroma throughout the hall. In this moment you are one with the Sacred, within and without. It is part of you, part of your spirit, part of the world, and part of the universe. Accept this unity; release yourself to it.

Stay with your God/dess until you know it's time to leave (trust me when I say, you will simply *know* this). Then visualize yourself leaving the room, locking it again, and returning the way from which you came. Know, however, that the key to the Sacred is always with you and part of you when you need it again. Make notes of your experience.

Cleansing and Purification

This meditation is useful for stress relief, improved health, psychic self-defense, and spiritual purification. I suggest you try this one lying down on a firm, comfortable surface.

See yourself as you lie presently, except your body seems to be translucent. Inside your skin, instead of bones and blood, every inch is filled with warm, yellow sand. At your toes there appear two plugs. Lean forward for a moment, take them out.

Slowly, almost imperceptibly, the sand begins to drain from your feet. With it, all your tension, anxiety, sickness, frustration, and negativity also seep away. From your ankles, your calves…your knees…your thighs…your hips…your waist…your hands…your arms…your shoulders…your neck…and finally, your head. The body's shell is now empty.

Above you, imagine a pure, sparkling light appearing. It pours down like a waterfall, moving from head to toe over your body's shell, until your skin shines like the light itself. Slowly you begin absorbing the light into the shell. It fills the shell from the toes upward, warming your ankles and calves, energizing your knees, thighs, hips, waist…. Empowering your hands, arms, and shoulders, and finally your head. You feel wholly well, renewed, refreshed, and filled with the light of spirit.

When you're ready, return to a normal level of awareness and make notes of your experience.

Communing With Spirit Guides

Spirit guides can take the form of humans, animals, and even plants. These powers come into our lives to counsel, protect, and guide us when our path becomes muddled, or when we get off track. This meditation is designed to help us seek out that guidance.

Begin your visualization in the same forest you imagined in the seasonal meditations. This time you remain as yourself and sit quietly under a tree. Take a moment to look around. What time of year is it? What's going on in the forest? Make a mental note of these things so you remember them later.

As you sit beneath the tree, let your mind wander a little and your inner vision blur. Focus on your desire to meet with a spirit guide, and why you need that being's aid. Try to keep this purpose in the back of your mind. Repeat the phrase "come to me" three times, while slowly changing the visualization.

To the right of you in the distance a portal begins to appear. It shimmers and shifts with all manner of lights and the wind within it seems to sing an old, familiar song. This continues for a while, until out of the center your guide will appear.

The guide will either stay where it is or come to you and communicate about the matter in your heart. This communication may not be verbal—you might feel it, or sense it telepathically. Observe everything the guide does and pay close attention to what it says until it leaves.

As your guide departs, remember to thank it, then return yourself to normal awareness. Make notes of everything in as much detail as possible in your journal and review them later for insight.

Facing the Shadows of Self

We all have our dark sides—those parts of ourselves that aren't as proverbially good as they might be. Many times we try to hide this aspect of self from ourselves, pretending it doesn't exist. But it does, and avoiding that truth can be detrimental to personal and spiritual development. This meditation helps us face our shadows and turn them into something positive.

Visualize yourself in your bedroom. Get up from where you are and go to the closet. Something rattles within and paces back and forth like a trapped animal. Slowly reach forward and crack open the door. Inside you find an outline of yourself, but it's shadowy and murky, like dirty water. It continues to pace, not really noticing your presence.

Look at this shadow and name it out loud. To know something's true name is to have power over it—which means you have control over this part of self as of *now*. Take the shadow in hand by the shoulders. Look at it closely, then give it a hug. Love is a powerful tool to banishing negativity. Now step back a bit, reach down into the shadow from its head...keep reaching and reaching. As you do, the shadow will compact so that eventually you'll reach its feet. Grab hold of these and shake the shadow inside out, like a pair of socks. When you do, it will turn into the most beautiful, blazing light imaginable.

When you face your fears and negativity and willfully wish to "turn" them around, you can! Hug this transformed light-self and absorb it into your being, then slowly return to normal aware-ness. Make notes of your experience.

Integrating Positive Attributes

Return once more to your spiritual forest. Find any spot that looks inviting and sit down. Before you, imagine a caterpillar creeping closer. It stops at your feet and begins to enclose you in a cocoon.

Before the cocoon closes completely, see yourself throwing out a symbol of those ideas and habits that you no longer need or desire. These have no place in nature's transformation chamber. Now let the caterpillar complete its task, enclosing you in glis-tening silence.

The cocoon around you shimmers with shifting light. It feels safe and secure. While you are here, begin repeating "Om" using a long, full breath. Do this three times. Next, say "I am" three times using a similar breath. Finally, add a word or short phrase that rep-resents the positive attribute(s) you want to add to the end of the phrase "I am" (such as "I am healthy"). Repeat this phrase thrice.

Your words echo in the chamber and throughout the chrysalis, until the vibrations fill your skin, bones, cells...your very soul. The vibrations continue to rise. The chrysalis starts to shake and crack. Finally it bursts open and you see yourself emerging from within with wings. These spiritual wings allow you to soar, to achieve, to know success. Let them take you where they will until you're ready to return to normal awareness. Make notes of your experience in your journal.

Spiritual Energizing

This visualization is designed to energize a depleted, weary spirit, but by changing the color of light used, it has many other applications. For example, substituting green light can improve health, well-being, and encourage personal growth. Yellow light aids creativity, pink light improves friendship and self-love, and blue light is peaceful.

Return to the spiritual forest, but instead of stopping here, keep walking until you find a small, well-worn path through the trees and up a hillside. Your feet know the way well and seem to take you upward without effort or thought. Ahead you can see a cave, shrouded in fog. As you get closer, the fog parts as if to welcome you, then closes behind, leaving you in total privacy.

The inside of the cave is lined and illuminated with crystals of all colors. Take a red one and a purple one from the wall and let them light your way to the center. Further in, and deeper down, the cave opens up. In the center of this area you'll find a large pool filled with pure, white light.

Stop at the edge of the pool and gently toss in the two crystals you carry. As they touch the water, the white light is joined by concentric circles of red and purple, swirling and dancing in the pool. Remove your clothes and wade in.

As you do, the swirls reach and embrace you, connecting themselves to each of your chakras. Through them energy pulses, revitalizing your spirit and drawing you ever closer to the source. This energy will continue to flow, filling every atom in your body, until you decide to withdraw.

Pick up the crystals from the bottom of the pool before you go, and put them back in the wall on the way out. They will remain there for your next visit. As you walk away, allow your awareness to return to normal, then note your experiences.

Note that if you go to the energy pool with other goals, you may want to change the chosen crystals or add affirmations or other vocalizations while you're in the light-water to support that goal.

Children's Meditations

> The clue of our destiny, wander where we will, lies at the foot of the cradle.
>
> —Jean Paul Richter

Not surprisingly, children have a very hard time meditating. They're easily distracted. Nonetheless, short meditations can prove very beneficial to children, especially those who are slightly hyper or who experience attention deficit disorder. Even a minute or two of thoughtfulness gives these children an opportunity to regulate themselves in a quiet, safe environment. In these moments, all the noise and activity of the outside world cannot influence them.

Additionally, meditation helps children discover themselves and their spiritual path over time. Even brief two- to five-minute meditations increase a child's natural connection to Spirit. Until a child gets older, you'll probably have to sit and walk her through these (they're written for reading out loud). Here your voice will become a mentor; a steady, guiding force in helping the child achieve her goals. And, since most children have vivid imaginations, it's easy for them to follow the imagery you create with words.

Afterward, it's a good idea to talk to the child about her experience. This helps with the integration process and gives her a chance to ask about symbols or feelings she didn't understand.

Confidence and Self-Control

Children frequently suffer from poor self-images and struggle with self-control. Most of this stems from peer pressure and youthful outlooks. Nonetheless, both situations can leave a child feeling sad or frustrated. This meditation is designed to help children feel more self-governed and self-assured.

Close your eyes and relax. Shake out your hands and arms, then let them rest. Shrug you shoulders, then let them rest. Now, I want you to imagine yourself as a tree. Your back is the tree's trunk. It's strong and has roots that reach way down into the earth. Your arms are branches with leaf fingers that touch the sky.

While you're standing in the woods, the wind picks up. The tree's branches move, dancing with it, but the trunk stays firm. Next comes a storm. The winds sound angry and try to push you every which way. Your trunk still stays firm. Your roots hold you, hugging the earth with every ounce of strength.

So even when other kids yell or push, even when fear or doubt seem to be winning...those roots are there for you. They connect you to the earth and to others so that you can stand strong and stay in control, no matter what you have to face. When you feel weak or scared, think of the tree and let it give you strength [bring the child back to normal awareness].

Health

Being stuck in bed actually affords a good opportunity to practice guided meditations with a child. It will also inspire sound sleep. This is one example where health is equated with a bandage that also encourages rest.

Close your eyes and imagine that you're in a large pool of warm, bubbly water. You're floating effortlessly on top of the water, which is glittery like stars. The glitter seems to tickle and warm your skin, like a fuzzy shirt might.

As you float, part of the glitter slowly takes a solid form—one piece at a time like a puzzle. The shape is a bandage, but it sparkles like dew. The bandage moves to you and wraps _____ [fill in with the region of the body effected, for example if it's a chest cold, the bandage encompasses the chest; if a broken leg, it would wrap the leg]. As it does, any discomfort begins to fade away, and you feel very sleepy and dreamy. Say, "I am healthy, I am well" with me [repeat this three times at least]. The waves rock you back and forth, back and forth, back and forth, gently and slowly [repeat this part of the visualization until the child seems really relaxed or falls naturally asleep].

Light Within

Children have a very simple concept of God, and it's one that should be fostered along with an understanding of spiritual energy. This meditation accents both.

Get comfortable and watch the flame of the candle. See how it twists, turns, and dances. Watch this until you can imagine it clearly with your eyes closed, then close your eyes.

See the flame hovering over the area of your heart. Slowly the flame comes closer to your skin, but it doesn't burn you at all. It's just warm and tingly. Next, the flame begins to twirl clockwise. It spins around and around more quickly until it goes into your heart—just like water spins into a drain. As it does, you feel very special and filled with energy. The flame inside is warm like before, but fills your body.

This flame is your soul, what makes you unique, and it's part of the Great Spirit. It is always inside of you—to give you strength and hope when you need it most. Whenever you feel bad, think about that flame and see it dancing happily. You'll start feeling happier, too [bring the child back to normal awareness].

Protection

The world being what it is, children need spiritual protection too. They're bombarded every day with images and thoughts that aren't necessarily positive or life-affirming. This visualization helps give them what I call the "hamster ball" of protection that they can easily see any time.

See yourself in your mind just as you are now. Above your head the sun is shining brightly. As it shines, the beams of light seem to pour down and begin forming a ball around you. More and more light pours into the ball until a shimmering circle surrounds you—above your head, below your feet, to the right, to the left, in front of you, and behind you.

Inside this sphere you feel totally safe. Nothing bad can reach you in here. Anything bad will bounce right off the wall of the circle and back to where it came from. So any time you feel scared, or like someone's trying to hurt you, see this circle and repeat "I am safe" three times. This will protect you [bring the child back to normal awareness].

These three meditations are good examples to use in designing others for the children in your life. Use imagery from favorite books or television programs in the meditations if it helps them relate better and focus on the goal or need. Other places you may find surprisingly good imagery is in comic books, coloring books, videos, children's toys, and music.

Meditations for Earth Healing

> If you wish to know the divine, feel the wind on your face and the warm sun on your hand.
>
> —Buddha

The power of meditation and visualization to generate earth healing should not be underestimated. Humankind has to be able to think globally before we can act globally. Meditation can encourage that broader perspective. In this case, the visualizations are designed to help the individual better relate to a large scope, and also to extend energy to the earth through will-directed imagining.

Earth Awareness

For this particular exercise there is no visualization. Go to a natural spot where you can sit quietly for several hours (the longer the better). Wear comfortable clothing. Close your eyes and go through basic relaxation exercises. When you feel ready, just sit with your eyes closed and extend all your senses.

What do you smell? What do you feel on your skin? What can you hear? What do you taste in the air? What can you figuratively see on the edge of your awareness with the eyes of spirit? Take your time, mentally noting odd sensations, unique sounds, and silences. Later, make notes on all of this in your journal.

If you make this meditation a weekly practice, you'll quickly find yourself becoming far more aware of, and attuned to, Earth's wonders.

Gaia's Body

Becoming aware of Gaia's body means to see yourself and all things as part of a great network. This visualization stresses that network.

Return to your sacred forest again, but this time remain as yourself. Sit down someplace comfortable and go through the relaxation exercise. When you feel totally at ease, visualize strands of different colored yarn extending out from your hands, your feet, your heart, and your head in all directions. These strands have different textures, too. As they touch trees and rocks and people, the strands bend, change color, or alter their texture, and weave themselves together into a web in which you are the center point.

Now, take yourself out to gaze at this web from a higher perspective, as if floating on a cloud. From here you can see the strands weaving together to form a familiar picture, but the images aren't clear. As before, each strand that touches another is somehow changed by that contact, and the picture transforms. Take a moment to follow your own strands to see how they affect all things.

Take yourself out even further, this time into space. Now you can see the tapestry's picture perfectly—it is the earth. Even more so, now you notice that the strands do not end in the atmosphere, but reach out to touch the moon, other planets, and continue out into the farthest reaches of the universe. Once again follow your strands—come to know yourself as a citizen, not only of Earth, but of this great expanse of beauty. See how important the strands of your life are to creating the tapestry. From this perspective, send thoughts of love and peace along your strands and watch the ripple effect this has on the whole image. Linger here as long as you wish.

Finally, return to the place where you first sat. Slowly retract your life's strands into yourself. They will naturally unravel. When you feel ready, return to a normal level of awareness and make notes of your experiences.

Gaia's Mind

As mentioned in the last chapter, we are the mind of Gaia. In this meditation you will be learning how to tap into thoughts and ideas that always exist in the communal consciousness of humankind (or the "collective unconscious," as Jung called it). The purpose of such contact is several fold. It can help you in understanding patterns in your life and the lives of those around you. It can improve divinatory efforts and it can enhance your ability to send out positive thought forms (energy) during spells or rituals for humankind's betterment and your own.

Walk into the spiritual forest and along the path that resides there. On the right side of the path, just off a ways, you'll notice an old well built from wood and stones. It's decorated with flowers and tiny white blossoms are blooming at its base. Walk over to this well.

If you look down into the well you can see blue-white light that swirls clockwise. Other small hints of color fill the light like fireflies. There's a bucket here and a handle that you can lower it with—so let the bucket down. As you do, repeat a word or phrase that represents the insights you seek. You'll notice the light's color shifting slightly to mirror the mood of that request.

Once the bucket is filled, pull it up and drink every last drop of the light. It's cool, yet warming—and seems to contain hints of your favorite flavors. It satisfies you and leaves you feeling totally energized and alert. This is a good time to linger at the well and mull over the situation or concept you wanted to emphasize. Make mental notes of any insights you receive, then slowly return to normal awareness and transfer these ideas into your journal.

Gaia's Spirit

Gaia's spirit is hurting. It's taken some pretty deep blows from the general lack of awareness on our part. The purpose of this visualization is to use a spiritual vision of the earth to send out positive energy that can become a healing balm.

If possible, perform this meditation outdoors, sitting on the ground. Having direct contact with soil improves the channeling of energy. In your mind's eye, imagine seeing the earth from space, slowly spinning in the light of the sun. Around it, the earth's aura (its atmosphere) glimmers dimly. There are signs of life and hope, but they've grown faint.

As you watch this, think of all the best things you hope for this planet and its residents—peace, love, joy—and extend your hands toward the earth's aura. Channel your feelings, your hopes, your love, through your hands in the form of silvery glitter that pours into the atmosphere. If it helps, verbalize these feelings. Pour out as much of this compassionate glitter as you can.

As you do, you will notice the earth's aura brightening a little. The glitter scatters and disperses itself evenly across the planet with every raindrop and sunbeam. Your love is now part of the earth's spirit and will remain there to bless it. Linger as long as you wish, then return to normal awareness and make notes of the experience.

Meditations for the New Millennium

> Behold how good and how pleasant it is when brethren dwell together in unity.
>
> —Psalm 133

One-World Thinking

It will be difficult to achieve global transformation without first thinking on a broader scale. The purpose of this meditation is to begin developing that perspective.

Begin with your relaxation exercise. When you're done, think of one decision that you recently made. Think of the ways that that decision affected you. Now, how did it affect the people around you—your family, friends, acquaintances? Might that decision have affected people you don't even know? If so, how?

Extend this line of thinking even farther. If the decision affected people you don't know, is it possible that it may also eventually affect situations along life's network that you can't see directly? Mentally try to follow the web that your decision created to see how far-reaching one person's actions really are. You'll be quite surprised by the outcome. When you've taken the thought process as far as you can, return to normal levels of awareness and make notes.

Use this meditation in the future when trying to determine the best possible action to take in any situation. Follow the webs created by each option to their most logical conclusion and that should help you make a positive decision.

Peace and Harmony

Stillness is something we know little of in this world. It is rarely quiet or calm, yet stillness in one's spirit is necessary before we can really hear and understand the voice of the Sacred. The purpose of this meditation is to encourage stillness and peace within so we can manifest it without.

Go through your pre-meditation exercise. This time, however, spend a great deal more time listening. Listen to your heartbeat and know it as your personal rhythm. Listen to the way your breath mingles with that rhythm, creating music that is wholly you.

Try not to think of anything else during this meditation. Empty your mind of everything but silence. Let nothing linger there, except for peacefulness. Find the place of stillness that lies within your mind and soul. There is no rushing here—no time, no space—just you and the Sacred.

Stay as long as possible in this mental space. When you find yourself getting irresistibly distracted, keep trying for another minute or two then return to normal awareness and make your notes. It takes practice to be able to keep this meditation going for longer periods, so don't get frustrated on your first (or tenth) try.

Spiritual Awakening

In Wicca we regard life as one journey among many that helps us attain enlightenment—to become one with the Sacred. Like lost children, we wander through our incarnations not certain what's missing or what we have to learn. This meditation is designed to accent our spiritual quest by awakening the ancient soul within us—the soul that remembers our past lives and learning. By reconnecting with this soul we can often obtain perspectives that help in spiritual development, especially when the road gets bumpy.

After your relaxation exercise, visualize yourself as you are, but filled with light. Each part of your body radiates different colors and textures that shift with your breathing and heartbeat. Direct your attention to the area in which your heart resides. Instead of a muscle, you'll see a vibrant flame that's twisted in the shape of a strand of DNA. This is the flame of your soul. Look closely at this power—along each bend and twist is one of life's experiences…a memory. They're all here.

As you watch, the flame becomes larger and larger. It overshadows the image of your light-body and becomes the only thing in your vision. Now, if you look at the twists, they appear a bit like window frames, each of which has a lock. Think about what it is you want to remember, a fear you wish to better understand, or an insight you want to gain. As you do, reach out. Let your inner voice guide your hand to the right window and open it.

Look through this window and make a mental note of what you see there. It might be a literal memory. There may be symbols, colors, shapes, or whatever. No matter what you see, remember it. This vision has direct significance to what's going on in your life right now, and your question. Stay in the window long enough to see everything there, then close it again knowing you can find this same window any time you need to.

At this point, the soul flame shrinks back to its normal size and you can return to normal levels of awareness. Make notes of your experience and consider the vision's significance in the days ahead. A dream key or any book of symbolism may help you better understand the images.

Universal Brotherhood

As humankind's mind grows, the earth begins to seem like a very small place indeed. There are hundreds of worlds outside this solar system...and we keep wondering if we are alone. I do not believe so. An important part of living in the new millennium will be continued space exploration—a reaching out to the universe and becoming aware of our place in it. This meditation is designed to send out positive, welcoming thoughts to other beings who may, like us, be looking for friends in the vastness.

Go outside, preferably in a place far removed from city lights and noise. Sit down at night beneath a starry sky and start your pre-meditation preparations. When completed, stare into the sky. Consider the wonder of it—the thousands of points of light and energy. When you start feeling dreamy, close your eyes, but keep a vision of the stars in your mind's eye.

Back up from the vision a bit and see the night sky like a dark pool filled with stars. Let yourself fall into this immenseness; dive into the pool expectantly. As your body touches the darkness, it transforms into light. You are now a star, too—your spirit is light among all the other lights of the sky. It beams brightly from your heart and shines on anyone looking.

Reach out with your arms of light. They'll go as far as you can imagine. Think loving, peaceful, welcoming thoughts. Hug the universe—let it know your hopes. Let anyone who might be listening know that you are a child of the universe seeking others of a like mind. Stay here as long as you wish, sensing the true magnitude of the universal spirit, then return to normal awareness and make your notes.

We cannot know for certain what our future holds. But, by thinking about our actions, by monitoring our thoughts, and consciously working for change, we can at least create a solid foundation where spirituality walks hand in hand with everyday life. This is a necessity that our ancestors understood and one that we need to reclaim to empower our magic and meditations for the new millennium.

4

Charms, Amulets, Talismans, Fetishes

> The best preparation for the future is the present well seen to, and the last duty done.
>
> —G. MacDonald

Early humans worshiped trees, the wind, and other aspects of nature, believing them to have powerful, in-dwelling spirits. As time wore on, this veneration shifted slightly. Shamans and wise people blessed and distributed natural objects such as magical charms and talismans, feeling that the power within them could (and should) be transported with an individual. The applications for these charms and amulets spanned the scope of human needs and desires—to protect, heal, draw love, increase luck, improve crops, motivate prosperity, and enhance spiritual insight, to name just a few.

The use of charms, amulets, talismans, and fetishes is still quite common in Wicca for several reasons. First, Wiccans agree with our ancestors, believing that natural objects house energies that can be directed and used for our welfare. From time to time, science has validated this belief, such as discovering that quartz crystals can run watches! Crystals house natural power, which science found a way to release. The magical practitioner does similarly, only we use willpower and metaphysical techniques to direct the object's energy.

Second, natural items are easy to obtain, easy to carry, and have strong symbolic value to which nearly anyone can relate. Rocks, for example, symbolize longevity and endurance. So someone feeling weak might carry a charged rock (see The Creation Process on page 90) to help generate strength. Trees represent the need for stability and roots, combined with the value of flexibility. So, someone with a tendency to daydream might put a leaf in their shoe to remind them to keep one foot on the ground. These are simplistic illustrations, but that's also their beauty. Nature's lessons and representations don't have to be complicated to be powerful, and they will remain so long into the future if we guard the earth diligently.

What's What

To love is the great Amulet that makes the world a garden...
—Robert Louis Stevenson

The word *charm* comes from the Latin *carmen*, meaning "song." Charms, therefore, have some type of verbal component, which in some cases, can actually act as the charm in itself. The words and objects bound together in a charm create magical power to improve good fortune, protect from evil, and gain affection. This last purpose is why we still call charismatic people "charming."

The word *amulet* comes from the Latin *amuletum*, meaning "to preserve." Amulets are actually a class of charm, designed out of metals, stones, plants, or sacred words. In ancient times mages often prepared these during auspicious moon signs or hours to increase the amulet's potency.

The exact elements of an amulet depends on its final purpose. All amulets, however, protect the bearer from evil influences or encourage positive energies. Numerous examples exist today, such as the little tokens people hang in their cars to keep them safe during travel, and even perhaps the lucky rabbit's foot.

The word *fetish* originates from the Portuguese *feitico*, meaning "sorcery." Fetishes are also a subclass of charm, often being made in the image of a Divine persona. The power of the fetish comes from the being it represents, or the Sacred power invoked during its creation. Generally speaking, when a person uses a fetish, it is burned or ritually destroyed in some manner to release the power of the token.

Finally, the word *talisman* comes from the Arabic *tilsam*, meaning "a magical figure." The thing that sets talismans apart from other tokens is that they are *always* created under specific astrological conditions, and often bear the image of a constellation, a planetary emblem, or other celestial objects. Talismans also protect their bearers from evil and disaster.

Originally, all such objects were made from natural components. Today, and looking to the future, however, we have many more options available. Numerous man-made items have the potential to become magical charms because of their durability and symbolic value. For example, an old key might be blessed and charged, then carried to open the path for love. An extra die or piece from a board game could be pocketed for luck. A match might become a charm to improve the "heat" in a relationship, or a pen could become a component in a creativity amulet for a writer.

Really, the selection for charm components is nearly limitless— as long as the chosen item represents your goal and is easily placed or carried where desired. So, while divination offers insight, prayer provides attitude, and meditation encourages awareness, charms offer us the flexibility to blend technology with magic in the new millennium.

The Creation Process

Invention is a kind of muse.

—John Dryden

Many examples of effective charms, amulets, talismans, and fetishes follow in this chapter. If you want to personalize these materials or make one for a purpose not listed herein, some guidelines will help you. First you need to find a suitable symbolic object. Note that "object" can also mean a piece of paper with the goal written upon it (this is especially true of charms).

SEVEN BASIC STEPS FOR MAKING CHARMS

1. Find an object that somehow represents your goal by its shape, color, or other quality.
2. Cleanse the object.
3. Charge the object (this is especially true of talismans).
4. Bless the object by calling on a personal deity or another Sacred power appropriate to your goal.
5. Work during auspicious astrological phases, if desired. (This is necessary for talismans.)
6. Create the charm using spells, incantations, or any other metaphysical methods that will empower it for use.
7. Carry it with you regularly, or put it where the energy will do the most good.

In considering what item(s) should become part of your charm, the final use of the token is of utmost importance. A token for your garden will need to weather the elements. Tokens for children need to be durable and nontoxic. Charms and amulets for pets need to be similarly safe and resistant to wear and tear.

I generally suggest you keep personal charms small. That way you can easily carry a variety with you to meet almost any need as it arises. Don't overlook the potential in clothing either. A tie can bind magic in its knot, a scarf might be empowered as an amulet for health, and perfume or cologne can become a love charm. Get creative!

Second, after you've found the central object, it needs to be cleansed of any residual energy. Cleansing leaves you with a spiritually clean tool into which you can put the energies desired (see Charging, below). To purify your token, pass it through the smoke from a purgative incense (like frankincense, cedar, or pine). Alternatively, soak it in salty or soapy water. If these options won't work because of the medium's sensitivity, visualize the object being filled with pure, white light that pushes out any unwanted vibrations.

Third, charge your token. Charging equates to filling the token with energy that's sympathetic to your goal. For matters of logic, reasoning, power, health, leadership, and the like, leave the token in sunlight for several hours. The sun is associated with masculine attributes and the conscious mind. For matters of intuition, nurturing, psychism, emotions, inner transformation, and the like, leave the token in moonlight for several hours. The moon is associated with feminine attributes and the subconscious or psychic mind. While the token charges up, you can chant, pray, or recite spells over it if you wish. This improves magical potency.

Step four is blessing. This usually takes the form of a deeply sincere prayer. Effectively, a blessing puts the token before the Sacred Powers with a stated purpose and requests that Divine favor be bestowed on the object and its purpose. By definition, a blessing is necessary for fetish creation, but optional for other charms.

Step five is also optional for all charms except talismans—that of working during auspicious astrological phases. Every hour of the day, each day of the week, every phase of the moon, and each sun sign can influence a charm's creation. For example, it might be best to make a charm to draw love during a waxing moon so love "grows." Or, you could make a talisman for improved judgement when the moon is in Sagittarius. In and of itself, timing won't make or break your magical work, but it certainly can help it along. A good astrological calendar will assist you in finding harmonic working times along with the chart below.

Now you are ready to finish the charm. The methods for completion depend on the object's use and your personal spiritual path. For example, the charms in this chapter have incantations that energize them because verbal components were important to traditional charm creation. Use the techniques shown here as a guide to which you add your vision and inventiveness for meaningful and powerful results.

THEMATIC CORRESPONDENCES

MOON

Full Moon: maturity, fulfillment, mastery
Waxing Moon: growth, integration, progress
Waning Moon: banishing, decreasing, halting
Dark Moon: rest, peace
Moon in Aries: enthusiasm, loyalty, sincerity
Moon in Taurus: failthfulness, affection
Moon in Gemini: versatility, improved perspective
Moon in Cancer: devotion, thrift
Moon in Leo: magnetism, romance, honesty
Moon in Virgo: generosity, recognition
Moon in Libra: grace, sociability, affection
Moon in Scorpio: pride, zeal
Moon in Sagittarius: idealism, liberation
Moon in Carpricorn: dignity, passion
Moon in Aquarius: detachment, optimism
Moon in Pisces: instinct, sentiment

SUN

Dawning Sun: new beginnings, hope
Noonday Sun: health, blessings, luck
Setting Sun: endings, completion
Sun in Aries: diligence, determination
Sun in Taurus: persistence, tenacity, friendship
Sun in Gemini: sensitivity, change, flexibility
Sun in Cancer: imagination, security
Sun in Leo: generosity, leadership, confidence
Sun in Virgo: levelheadedness, responsibility
Sun in Libra: charm, diplomacy, communication
Sun in Scorpio: shrewdness, keen-mindedness
Sun in Sagittarius: enthusiasm, tolerance, adventure
Sun in Capricorn: loyalty, practicality, accomplishment
Sun in Aquarius: creativity, self-expression
Sun in Pisces: kindness, love, empathy

Once created, keep the token in an appropriate place. If you've made it for yourself, carry or wear it regularly. If made for your home or the people who live there, put it near the hearth—the heart of a home. For friends, create the charm in the form of a decorative accent piece and give it to them as a gift with a note of explanation. For pets, put the token where they sleep or eat. For children, stuff it in a pillow or sew it into a coat pocket. This way the charm can radiate magic where it will do the most good.

Seasonal Tokens

So then the year is repeating its old story again…

—Goethe

These amulets and talismans are designed with the theme of each season in mind, specifically to amplify the energy of that season and to integrate specific attributes into our life appropriate to the season.

Spring

Spring is the time of renewal—renewed hope, renewed joy, renewed energy. With this upbeat energy comes thoughts of romance, playful relationships, and happy friendships. This charm accents those thoughts with magic.

Begin with a heart. This can be made out of anything as long as you can carry it with you easily. Also have ready a small feather and a mixture of rose water and marjoram tea. Take your heart in one hand (don't overlook the symbolism in this action) and visualize it being filled with pink-white light that nearly prances with delight. Take the feather in your other hand and dip it into the water mixture. Apply it to the heart saying,

> *Powers of Spring, let my soul sing!*
> *With joy let it dance; renew romance!*
> *Tickle my heart; playfulness impart!*

Carry this token as close as possible to your heart until you feel yourself filled to overflowing with happiness, and you see your relationships improving. At this point, either share the charm with someone who needs it, or put it away to use again next spring.

Summer

Summer seems to come with a flurry of activity (at least in my home). People are visiting, vacationing, exercising, and so forth. All this takes a lot of personal energy, which sometimes seems lacking when you want it most. This talisman will help.

To begin, you will need any small gold-colored object. A yellow-gold AAA battery is an excellent choice because it can symbolize the "holding" of energy. On a bright, sunny day go outside just before the clock strikes noon. As it begins to chime, hold the battery (or other object) up to the light reciting the following incantation on the first six tolls:

> *With the toll of one, this spell's begun.*
> *Come the chime of two, the magic's true.*

> *Come the ring of three, energy to me.*
> *Come the toll of four, the power to store.*
> *Come the chime of five, the magic's alive.*
> *Come the ring of six, the energy—affix.*

As the clock strikes six more times, visualize the golden rays of the sun being absorbed by your token. Carry this with you any time you feel your inner reserves waning. Touch it lightly saying "The magic's alive" when you want to release a little energy. After six uses, you should recharge your token in sunlight again.

Fall

The time of the harvest is come. What projects or characteristics have you been working on in your life that you'd like to see manifest? Decide among these, and make this fetish to help the manifestation process along.

You will need a small amount of rich soil, a portable container, and a symbol of the project or attribute you've chosen for this token (this needs to fit in the container). Place your hand on the rich soil and say,

> *Ops, Goddess of the harvest and success,*
> *See my efforts to _____ [describe your goal]*
> *Help me to reap what I have diligently sown and tended.*
> *Energize this fetish with your presence*
> *So that like the earth, I too may harvest _____.*
> *So be it.*

Note that this fetish can be empowered further by making it on December 19 (Ops's traditional festival date) and then putting it away for when you need it the following autumn.

Winter

Winter seems to be the time when thoughts naturally turn to chicken soup and warm blankets. Chill in the air or not, however, no one wants to be in bed sick during the holiday season. Make this healthful bundle of amulets to help keep those winter aches and pains away.

Begin with a box of bandages. Leave these in the light of the sun for three hours (three is the number of body-mind-spirit). At the end of the third hour, take the box in hand, focusing on your intention to stay healthy, and say:

> *Not for love, nor for wealth*
> *My wish today is one for health.*
> *Healthy body, healthy mind*
> *By these words all sickness I bind!*
> *When 'ere these tokens are kept with me*
> *Banish all illness; bring vitality!*

Keep the package in a secure location and put one or two of the bandages in your wallet. When you start feeling run down, apply the bandage to symbolically "apply" the magic.

Thematic Tokens

Give me an amulet that keeps intelligence with you.

—Ralph Waldo Emerson

Every day brings different situations, each of which highlights specific needs or goals in our lives. Charms and amulets represent one way to keep an assortment of magical powers on hand for any occasion. Effectively, each token created puts Universal energy in our pockets, like a battery just waiting to be activated when it's most needed.

All-Purpose Bundle

The idea behind this token is to make a very portable charm that binds together protective, healthful, prosperous, lucky, and peaceful energy into one spot. To make it you will need a small drawstring pouch on which you've painted the image of a pentagram.

In mystical traditions, this symbol represents the five elements and the spark of magic; it's also protective. You also need to gather together five tiny stones: one white (protection), one bright green (health), one dark green or gold (wealth), one yellow (luck), and one blue (peace).

On your birthday or another special occasion, take these in hand visualizing all the best things in life being yours. Put them in the pouch one at a time saying:

> *One for luck, two for wealth;*
> *Three for safety, four for wealth;*
> *Five—the magic shall never cease;*
> *Magic bound within, to bring me peace.*

Tie up the pouch and keep it with you frequently. When an occasion comes up that you need one of the energies in a specific stone, take it out and plant it in the ground so the magic can grow. Replace the stone later and recharge the entire collection.

Conscious Mind

When you need to think clearly and see things with an objective eye, make and carry this talisman. To begin, you'll need some caraway and celery seed that's been charged in sunlight for seven hours (completion) and a small gold-tone tin (gold accents the logical self). Place the seeds in the tin during the daytime, preferably at noon on a sunny day, saying:

> *Illuminate my mind.*
> *Let me see clearly, even things that seem elusive.*
> *When scattered around, chase back the shadows of uncertainty.*
> *When held close to my heart, reason impart.*

Carry this with you. Hold it in your hand when you feel your judgement is "iffy." Sprinkle some seeds from the container when you need to clarify an idea or situation right away. When you run out of seeds, refill the container and energize it again with the incantation.

Courage

The future meets us head-on with many challenges and demands. Some situations will require nothing less than a leap of faith to navigate victoriously. When these difficulties arise, courage becomes an ally for success. This disposable fetish is meant to motivate bravery in your heart at the moment when it's most needed.

Begin with a piece of plain white paper with the word *apprehension* written upon it in red. In the middle of the paper (where the word is written) place a dried oak leaf, some pepper, and some dried tobacco (unrefined). These items are all sacred to Mars, the god of war and bravery.

Think about overcoming your anxiety, pouring that feeling into the paper. Crumple up the paper fiercely, making sure the herb(s) are securely in the middle. Put this paper on a safe fire source so it ignites. Until it burns completely out, repeat this incantation:

> *Mars, let me take up your spear; banish my fears*
> *To face adversity—courage to me!*

Take the ashes and scatter a few to the winds to bear your wish to the heavens, plant some so the magic grows, and carry the rest. Release a pinch of ash to the earth whenever you need more courage.

Energy

There are moments when everyone needs a little pick-me-up, especially with today's hectic schedules. This talisman is created to provide improved energy when you find your feet dragging.

Begin by finding a small bottle with a secure top when the moon is in its waxing phase, or when the sun is in Taurus. In a pan place one cup of water, a tablespoon of honey, quarter teaspoon of vanilla extract, two or three sprigs of rosemary, a quarter-inch of bruised gingerroot, and a couple of allspice berries. Warm this over a low flame to create a heady tea. While it cooks, stir the mixture clockwise repeating the phrase, *"energy and power in this magical hour."*

Cool and strain the tea, adding two tablespoons of rum (this is a preservative). Pour the mixture into the bottle and cap it tightly. Keep any remainders in an airtight container and store it in a dark, cool place. Carry the portable bottle with you. Whenever you feel you need more energy either smell the blend (like aromatherapy) or take a sip. Dispose of it if it ever becomes cloudy.

Friendship

Good friends are a treasure beyond words. As the years go on, sometimes we drift apart from old friends and need to find new ones. When you wish to meet potential friends, or improve the quality of current friendships, make and carry this charm.

In a small pink cloth (or container), place some dried lemon peel, lemon seeds, and a sweet pea blossom. Tie this together saying,

> *Lemon zest makes this friendship the best.*
> *The flower I bind, new friends be mine!*

If you're going somewhere that you can meet new people, or to improve your relationship with someone you already know, take out a pinch of the peel and seeds and drop it just outside the door to release the magic. Refill and recharge when the peel and seeds are depleted. (Always keep the flower intact.)

Happiness

Happiness is a commodity of which everyone can use a little more. This amulet is designed to keep negativity at bay so that you can fill your life with more joy, and keep it strong. To make this, you'll need a sprig of fresh heather (check out a nursery for a houseplant) and a bowl of saltwater.

During a waning moon, dip the heather sprig in the saltwater and sprinkle it around your living space and around your body, moving counterclockwise. As you move, repeat this phrase: *"Turn away, turn away, all negativity kept at bay."* When you finish, break off a few of the flowers and place them in your shoe or wallet. This will bear the protective energy with you and draw a little extra luck and happiness your way.

Health and Well–Being

It's hard to accomplish anything physically, mentally, or spiritually when you're feeling under the weather. The purpose of this amulet is to give you a portable source of protection and defense that can be internalized when you feel yourself dragging.

Begin with a small tin of green–colored mints or other candies (green accents health). Leave this in sunlight for three hours (to emphasize well-being), and in the light of a waning moon for three hours (to "shrink" illness). Afterward, bless the candies saying:

> *Sweets contained by this tin*
> *Once through my lips, let the magic begin*
> *Manifest renewed health within.*

When your energy seems low, or you're feeling off, take one of the candies, repeat the incantation, then eat it to internalize your magic. Refill the container and charge as needed.

Love

Love makes the world go 'round, and it's not just the love between couples. It is the love between friends, between family members, between you and a pet project. No matter the outlet, however, love is an essential ingredient to human well-being. This charm is designed to draw more love into your life on a regular basis.

Gather together a pink or red cloth (approx. 4" ˇ 4"), a pink candle, matches, a peach pit, a length of string, and vanilla extract. Lay the cloth out in front of the lit candle with the peach pit in the center. Drop three drops of extract on the pit saying, "love for my body, love for my mind, love for my spirit."

Next, take the candle and let three drops of wax fall onto the pit saying *"Friendship, kindness, passion, come to me"* (note you can change the three facets of love here to something more personally desired). Tie up the cloth using the string and carry the token with you. Or, leave it near a fire source in your home to keep figurative warmth in your life

Luck No. 1

Luck is an elusive quality, and some people seem to have an abundance of it. The rest of us hope that a little will rub off on us! When your fortune seems to have taken a turn for the worse, try this fetish.

You'll need to find an egg timer or other small hourglass as a component. Take this in hand, imagining the sand as sparkling light and say:

> *Master of the Sands and Lady Fate*
> *Hear my prayer, bad luck abate.*
> *When this hourglass turns 'round*
> *Only good fortune shall abound!*

Turn the hourglass only once and let it do its work. Leave it in a safe place where it won't be tampered with until you need to change your luck again.

Luck No. 2

Instead of changing the present energies, this lucky talisman is designed to draw good luck to you (or you to it). The central component for this charm is any coin that bears the year of your birth on it. Also, have ready a small piece of dried orange rind and a bit of glue.

During a waxing moon attach the orange (which is a token of good fortune in China) to the coin with the glue saying:

> *The orange with coin is neatly bound*
> *So good luck will come around.*
> *Good luck to me, good luck I'll see!*

You may want to wrap the coin with a bit of natural fabric so the orange rind doesn't accidentally get knocked off when you're carrying the token. When you need luck quickly, touch the coin and recite the incantation.

Peace

For peace to come to our planet it has to start in each individual's heart. This fetish is designed to encourage inner peace by calling on the Roman Goddess of peace, Concordia. Her sacred token is an olive branch, so you will need an olive leaf for this token (check any stores that sell Greek culinary supplies).

If possible, prepare this fetish on January 16 or 22, March 30, April 1, or May 11—each date was a traditional festival day for Concordia. Take the olive leaf in hand, visualizing it filled with comforting, white light. When the leaf starts feeling warm in your hand, raise it to the sky saying:

Concordia,
See this, your symbol of peace and accord.
Bless and empower it that I might know harmony of body, mind and
*   spirit.*
So be it.

For extra symbolic value, wrap the leaf in a heart-shaped cloth (putting peace in your heart) and carry it with you always. When the time comes that the leaf has completely dried and crumpled into tiny bits, burn it to release peace in your home and make a new token to carry.

Prosperity

Prosperity is not just based on one's checkbook. It can be found in living well with whatever we have been given: our friends, our family, our health. Nonetheless, while money can't buy happiness, it certainly makes life less stressful. So when you want to improve your cash flow a little, or find creative ways to make the budget go further, make this charm.

For this you'll need a gold-toned portable container with a good lid, and some popcorn kernels, oatmeal, and cornflakes. Mix together the three grain crops (symbolizing abundance and sustenance) and put it in the container. When financial needs arise, take a pinch of this mixture and release it to the winds saying:

> *On the winds my wishes fly free.*
> *Return to me with prosperity!*

Keep your eyes and ears open for an opportunity to ease your burdens! Refill the container when it's empty.

Psychic Ability

Wiccan spiritual goals include developing our intuitive, psychic selves to the best of our ability. This isn't easy in a world where one is taught that "Seeing is believing." This talisman will help.

Gather a silver-toned key (the color of the moon, which is linked with intuitive ability), a white length of yarn or cord, and some steeped black tea. Put the key in the tea to charge it by the light of a full moon for seven hours. At the end of the seventh hour, pour out the tea to the earth as a libation. Hold the key up to the moon saying:

> *Lady Moon, Mother Moon, see this key.*
> *Let it release spiritual talents dormant within me.*

Put the key on the yarn or cord and wear it any time you're trying divination or other metaphysical activities where you need improved sensitivity. Perhaps use it as a pendulum!

Sleep

When the world gets chaotic and noisy, sometimes the one thing we really need (but can't always get) is a peaceful night's sleep. This talisman improves the restful energy in your bedroom. Begin with two four-inch square pieces of blue fabric sewn together on three sides. Into this pocket place two tbs. chamomile, one tbs.

hops, one tbs. lavender, two tbs. mint, one-half tsp. rosemary, and one-half tsp. thyme. Sew up the last edge of the pocket saying:

> *Thyme to keep nightmares away,*
> *Rosemary to sleep until day,*
> *Peppermint to bring sweet dreams,*
> *Lavender, peace within my pillow's seams,*
> *Chamomile to rest safe and sound,*
> *With each stitch, the magic's bound.*

Flatten out the sachet and put it inside your pillowcase on those nights when you need to get a decent amount of sleep. Dab periodically with essential oils or refill the herbs when the aroma wanes to keep the magic fresh.

Wisdom

Sound discernment and judgment help in almost every aspect of life. As we move bravely forward into the future, wise thought and action become more important to successful living. This charm helps keep wisdom with you on the Path of Beauty.

Begin with one-half cup of cornstarch and two tbs. of sage. Run this through a hand sifter saying:

> *Wherever I walk, let me find insight.*
> *Wherever I look, let me see truly.*
> *Whatever I listen to, let me hear fully.*
> *Wisdom be my guide.*
> *In my heart, always abide.*

Keep this in a handy container and dust your shoes with it on those days when you want a little extra sagacity as a companion.

Children's Tokens

You cannot teach a child to take care of himself unless you will let him try to take care of himself.

—H. W. Beecher

When we begin teaching children magic, using charms and amulets are among the easiest things for them to understand. Children are drawn to stones and plants quite naturally. I've often watched in amazement when children wander through science stores and pick out the exact stones suited to their personalities. This indicates an instinctive awareness of natural energies that making charms can augment.

Anti-Nightmare Blanket

Young children seem to share a common fear of the dark and often experience nightmares because of it. To offset this problem and give the child a greater sense of control, turn a favored blanket into a nightmare amulet.

To do this, sit with the child and his chosen blanket. Both of you hug it tight while holding each other. Let all your love pour into that cloth, and visualize it being filled with protective light. Bless the cloth together saying:

> *Things that go bump; the fears of the night*
> *All go away in Spirit's light.*
> *Magic in this blanket's seams*
> *Will bring only the best of dreams.*

Give him the blanket when he goes to bed or place it on top of his pillow so he can put his head on the loving, protective energy you've created together.

Attention Charm

Some children find it particularly difficult to sit still and pay attention at school. This little portable token can give them extra confidence and settle their spirits. Have the child make a bunch of paper book covers. When the covers are done, she can dab the four corners with a mixture of lavender and rosemary oil (peace and memory improvement) saying:

> *North and South, East and West,*
> *Help me do my very best!*

Teach the child to touch the four corners in the order given, and how to mentally recite the power phrase when she feels her mind wandering. When the aroma on the covers wanes, just add a little more oil and repeat the incantation to refresh the magic.

Character Candle

This is a great Saturday project. Ask your child to name one characteristic that he would most like to develop or improve upon (give him examples like being more patient, kind, helpful and so on). Choose a colored wax that accents that goal. For example, kindness might be pink, while patience is augmented by the color blue. Also, choose a corresponding aromatic oil and an easily carved emblem that represents the child's intent.

Melt the wax together. Let it cool a little bit, then add the aromatic oil. Pour this into an old milk carton with a wick attached by a paper clip. While the candle cools, have the child hold his hands over the top of it, and repeat a word or phrase that represents his goal. Using the aforementioned examples, he or she might say "When this light shines, I will be more kind," or "Patience I claim, within this candle's flame."

Once the candle hardens, dip the carton in warm water long enough to loosen the sides and unmold the candle. Help the child carve the symbol on its side. He can then put the candle in a safe place and take it out to light it when he feels the need, repeating the power phrase as the candle ignites (make sure he asks for your help in lighting the candle). The light signals the release of the magical energy placed within.

By the way, I know some families who make a similar candle (one per person) to signal the need to talk about something or as a silent way of asking for help. I think this is a terrific idea, especially in families that have trouble communicating effectively.

Courage Charm

Children have fears, many of which stem from highly active imaginations and a sense that they lack control in their lives. This charm is designed to help them feel stronger and self-regulated when fear seems to be winning.

On a day when the moon is waxing, or when the sun is in Leo, take a box of black-tea bags and have your child hold the box in the palm of her hand. She should imagine it being filled with a color of light she associates with courage (red is common). Then say together:

> *Courage within, let the magic begin.*
> *When placed in a cup, let courage erupt.*
> *When I drink the tea, there's courage in me!*

Give the child one tea bag to keep with her (possibly with a cup in her lunch box) so she can make the tea any time she wants to internalize the magic. Keep the other bags at home in an accessible place.

Healthy Vitamins

For this edible amulet, you'll need a container of children's vitamins. You and your child will be energizing these together so each day she can internalize the magic of wellness through a medium that emphasizes that goal (the vitamin).

If you want to add special timing to this, energize the vitamins in sunlight, which is considered healthful, or by a waning moon so any malady "shrinks." Visualize the vitamins being filled with spring-green light and repeat this incantation three times (for physical, mental, and spiritual health):

> *Good health to win, when taken within*
> *Sickness depart, good health impart.*

Have the child take one a day, repeating the power phrase with her as she does.

Love Bear

There's nothing like a huggable teddy bear (or other stuffed animal) to make younger children feel better when they're sad.

With this in mind, take a special stuffed animal and make it into a love charm that releases warm, comforting energy whenever the child needs it. This particular charm might be best fashioned when the sun is in Pisces to emphasize empathy and love.

Have the child hold the toy closely, hugging it tight. Wrap your arms around both the child and the toy, then say together:

> *This _____ [type of animal] of cloth has a magical heart.*
> *When I hold it tight, let the magic start.*
> *Love and peace bound inside,*
> *There the magic will forever abide.*

Sadness Scents

Find a small swatch of brightly colored cloth. With the child, place a pinch of marjoram, catnip, and lavender within. As you do this, repeat this incantation:

> *Marjoram and lavender keep sadness away.*
> *Catnip reminds me to laugh and play.*
> *Wrapped inside this cloth so bright,*
> *Joy to me, sadness take flight!*

Put the aromatic sachet in the child's underwear or sock drawer so the energy of joy goes with her each day with her clothing.

Study Talisman

As children get older and school studies become more difficult, studying seems like a chore. For children who have trouble concentrating on their lessons, this fetish should help.

Begin with four whole flower blossoms (any type of flower will do—this honors the Goddess invoked). You will also need a handful of rosemary (for conscious focus) and a portable container with a good lid. Have the child pluck the petals and put them in the container mixing them with the rosemary, while focusing on his goal. Hold your hands and the child's over the mixture and bless it saying:

Sarasvati, Lady of the mind and learning
Help keep my mind on my work.
When I get distracted, let the magic within this mixture
Get me back on track, and my focus sure.
Thank you.

Instruct the child to release a pinch of the mixture to the wind any time he feels really restless and unable to concentrate. This invokes Sarasvati's assistance and releases the magic.

Earth-Healing Tokens

The Great Spirit is the life that is in all things.

—Rolling Thunder

The earth-healing tokens presented here aren't portable like most amulets and charms but are created to effect the region in which they dwell. Like the standing stones and monoliths of the ancient world, these smaller magical signposts radiate energy outward to bless the earth around them.

Earth Awareness

One of the best ways to become more intimately aware of the earth is to work with it. For this charm, I suggest creating a small planter in which you place the seed of any long-lived flowering plant. As you put the seed in a rich soil womb say:

Seed of earth, sown with love
Seed of earth, nurtured with kindness
Seed of earth, grown with tolerance
Seed of earth, blossom with peace.

Make as many of these planters as you wish: Put one at home, one at the office, one at a friend's house—any place you feel it would help. Each time you tend the plant, you are also symbolically ministering to the earth, and learning more about its cycles.

Body of Gaia

As mentioned in the introduction to this section, ancient people created special gardens or stone circles to channel the earth's energies and bless the land. This talismanic garden does the same. Because not all readers have a lot of yard space, this is designed for indoors, but it can be expanded for an outdoor site.

Begin with a square box (a square represents the four corners of creation) that is filled with sand or soil. Also collect various colors of seeds or grains. These go on top of the sand or soil in sacred patterns. You can make any type of pattern you wish, so long as it represents a specific global goal in some way. Focus intently on that goal while you work.

For example, if making a mandala for earth healing, you might want to use white seeds patterned in a circle to represent the globe. Energize the pattern by working during a full moon (for wholeness) and chanting as you go. Let your inner voice guide you with regard to the completed pattern. Leave this in the soil or sand for at least seven days, reciting the chant you used in making it each time you see it. Then scatter the seeds to the earth to spread the magic.

Make a new pattern afterward and follow the same procedure so you have an ongoing magical center of energy that's directed to the earth.

Mind of Gaia

To accent the human awareness of earth's sacredness, use natural objects in and around your home that create a sacred space. In this case, bless and energize five stones, four of which represent the elements by their color (fire—red/orange, earth—brown/black, water—blue/purple, air—yellow/white). The fifth stone represents you.

Put the four elemental stones around the perimeter of your living space in the appropriate directional quarter (east—air, west—water, south—fire, north—earth). As you do, activate their energy by saying.

> *To the earth, into the ground*
> *Here to stay, the magic's bound*
> *To heal the earth and Gaia's mind*
> *Within this stone, the power bind*
> *To inspire peace, our wounds to heal*
> *By my words the magic's sealed.*

Repeat this incantation over each stone as its placed in the ground or around your home. Carry the fifth stone with you as a charm to motivate improvements no matter where you may be.

Spirit of Gaia

This charm is both beautiful and fun to create. Find a variety of crystal points that can easily be wrapped in wire. Wrap each one with copper (to transmit their energy) saying:

> *Ring out peace, sing of harmony that ne'er ceases*
> *A spell born with the wind, by the breezes.*
> *Begin healing power of my rhyme*
> *Saturate with magic this little chime.*

String all the points but one along a branch or a curtain rod using fishing line. This allows them to catch and scatter light, as well as knock together, making a crystalline wind chime that rings out the magical energy stored within. Keep the last crystal with you as an amulet for inspiring harmony with others.

New Millennium Tokens

> Vision looks inward and becomes duty. Vision looks outward and becomes aspiration. Vision looks upward and becomes faith.
>
> —Stephen S. Wise

Wiccan approaches change and adapt with the times. Looking ahead, I suspect more man-made objects and bits of technology will begin to be used in magic. This is a positive step: Technology doesn't have to be antithetical to spirituality if we apply it effectively and wisely. These charms are good examples of how to do just that.

Adaptation

Learning to bend and flow with a rapidly changing environment isn't always easy. Use this little fetish as a reminder of the value of flexibility, and to encourage more adaptability in your life.

All you need to begin is a rubber band or elastic hair band. Stretch it out while standing in a southerly wind saying:

> *Notos, God of the changing winds*
> *Bless now my spell, let the magic begin.*
> *Like this elastic, which bends and wraps,*
> *Teach me how to cope and adapt!*

Put the rubber band on a key ring or other regularly carried item to inspire flexibility, no matter the situation.

Car Talisman

For many, a car is nearly an indispensable necessity. When one breaks down, it causes all manner of difficulty at home and at work, thereby disrupting harmony. To help protect your car from mishaps, try this functional talisman.

Take a pair of jumper cables and charge them by sunlight for seven hours (for power). Then, come a waning moon, bless them saying:

> *Lady and Lord of adventure's road*
> *Always bring me safely home,*
> *Whether I travel near or far*
> *Protect and bless my little car.*

Put the jumper cables in your trunk. An alternative to cables is to similarly bless a tool kit.

Communication

Sometimes it seems difficult to catch up with the people with whom we most need to speak. They, like us, are busy, and everyone ends up playing telephone tag. When this happens, try using this charm.

Purchase a prepaid phone card in any amount you can use or easily afford. Hold it in your hands and visualize the person with whom you need to speak. Recite an incantation like:

> *Open the way; listen to what I must say*
> *The magical power works on the hour*
> *I will talk to* _____ [person's name] *today!*

Call the person once an hour, on the hour. You should reach them before the day is over. Afterward you can cleanse the card of that specific energy by passing it through incense smoke. Then use a new incantation to charge it again.

Conscious Mind

Of all modern symbols, computers come closest to representing human consciousness, but with greater clarity. So, when you find yourself in need of improved reasoning faculties, an old computer chip makes a great component. To obtain one, either save a bad chip from your own system or ask for one at a computer store.

Take the chip and sit with it beneath the light of a noon day sun. Dab it with a little rosemary oil (if available). Energize the chip with an incantation like:

> *Within my mind, let logic shine!*
> *The powers I behoove, help my memory improve!*

Have a friend or family member with a decent tool kit punch a hole in it for you so it can go on a key chain, or somewhere else that you can easily carry it.

Discernment

When it's time to take off the proverbial rose-colored glasses and see things clearly, grab a handy magnifying glass instead. Anoint this with a little spearmint essence or oil (for mental keenness) saying:

> *Through this glass, no falsehood may pass.*
> *When I look around, only truth shall be found.*
> *Within this glass so fine, discernment is mine.*

Look through the glass at papers or people when you need to see them more clearly, with the eyes of Spirit.

Frugality

Tightening one's belt and balancing the budget are things most workaday folks are quite used to. With so many wonderful adult toys available, it is sometimes hard to resist the call of the credit card. This amulet is designed to protect your finances and improve personal resolve when you feel tempted.

   Take a dollar bill and some plastic wrap. Fold the bill in thirds the long way once, then again saying:

> *Tucked neatly away, temptation shall stay.*
> *Folded three by three, prosperity to me!*

Put this inside the plastic wrap as symbolic preservative, then carry the token with you.

Negativity Amulet

In ancient times, people used reflective surfaces to "turn away" the evil eye and other mal-intended magic. A modern alternative is a piece of aluminum foil. It can reflect unwanted energy and positive light to neatly protect the bearer from harm and mischief.

Take a small scrap in hand and visualize it being filled to over-flowing with protective light. When the aluminum feels slightly warm in your hands say:

> *Negativity and evil kept firmly at bay,*
> *Goodness and light, forever to stay.*

Bundle up the aluminum foil into a small ball and carry it in a pocket, briefcase, or purse.

As you can see from this small sample, anything and everything has the potential for magic if you look at it with a creative, optimistic eye. This is the vision we need to carry and use in the new millennium in order to keep the Wiccan tradition alive and vibrant for yet another thousand years.

5

Spellcraft

The sound of music slumbers in the shell, till waked and
kindled by the master's spell; and feeling hearts, touch
them rightly, pour, a thousand melodies unheard before.

—Samuel Rogers

Spellcraft is a very ancient, will-driven art. By definition, spells
combine the elements of actions, words, components, and thoughts
into a kind of mini-ritual. A Wiccan chooses each spell element
carefully to create a specific type of energy (love, joy, prosperity,
health, luck, and others). The casting of a spell then generates,
releases, and directs the thematic energy. This power becomes a
motif in one's environment reaching ever outward to manifest the
magician's intention. So, while divination furnishes insight, prayer
influences attitude, meditation produces awareness, and charms
offer flexibility, spells create energy blueprints that can be used in
building a better magical future.

In early magical traditions our ancestors, not having interna-
tional supermarkets available, chose mostly backyard components

for their spells. Incantations were comprised of socially or culturally familiar words. And while some special timing might have been added for symbolism, generally people worked spells whenever the need arose. This type of folk magic, in its beautiful simplicity, blended everyday life and environmentally generated symbols with spirituality for very meaningful, and often potent, results.

Today, Wiccans continue to honor the art of spellcraft as one of the central techniques to our spiritual tradition. As in times past, heartfelt approaches to spellcraft that take into account personal realities and spiritual vision are by far the most popular. While some circumstances might benefit from highly ritualized spells, most of life's everyday needs can still be met using folk magic as a foundation. Why? Because folk magic bases its entire philosophy and methodology on one simple rule: If it's available, personally significant, and suitable to your intention, by all means use it! This makes folk magic one of the most flexible and adaptable of all Wiccan spiritual traditions, which also insures its longevity.

Props and Processes

> It [magic, witchcraft] was a reality that people in non-scientific ages struggled with...but they knew it.
>
> —Louisa Rhine

Before trying specific spells, it's helpful to understand the techniques and components that appear in many folk traditions, and those that Wiccans continue to use regularly. This way you'll have a basic pattern to follow in creating your own spells, or adapting those given herein. Most of the items and methods presented in this chapter have a timeless appeal that won't easily become obsolete, no matter our societal advances. But, as with all types of magic, I encourage you to follow your spiritual vision in what you try or use personally. Inevitably, following your inner voice always yields the best results.

Components

Think of components in spellcraft like the ingredients to a terrific recipe. You don't usually tinker with what works well, but you might want to make some minor adjustments to suit personal tastes. Spellcraft works similarly.

Everything in the world has various metaphysical associations and powers ascribed to it. These associations determine the potential ingredient list for a successful magical recipe. But, since Wicca strongly advocates personal vision and modification, each individual may chose a different ingredient from this list to make her spell more personal, meaningful, and spiritually fulfilling.

Certain components were, and are, popular in spellcraft because of their range of uses. A description of these common components, and practical ways to use them in your magical recipes, follow. As was the case with charms and amulets, natural components predominate this list, but nothing says we can't add man-made ones into the mix. What's most important is that each ingredient works harmoniously with the others in a spell, and that each ingredient makes sense considering the purpose of your magic. Where more modern and futuristic options are available for your consideration, they are so noted.

AROMATICS   Aromas activate our sense of smell, which can influence the outcome of magical procedures just like any other sensual input. That's one reason why the ancient temples often had incense burning. By using an aromatic in spellcraft you not only affect the vibrations in your own aura, but also the energy in the air wherever the aroma reaches, your magic can reach out and bless others, even without your knowledge!

Burning incense or herbs is but one option—an option that in the ancient world represented our prayers and wishes floating up to the Great Spirit. Another possibility is to dab scented oil around the room where you're working, or perhaps just put some on your tools. Decorate the sacred space with fresh flowers whose color and aroma accent your spell. Dust the carpets in a room with patchouli-scented baking soda to help you ground after working magic. Use personal perfume or cologne as one of the components in a love spell. Or, toss a cinnamon-scented cloth into the dryer with your clothes to draw luck to you, no matter where you may be. With a little creativity, the options are nearly endless!

CANDLES The flame of a candle represents the human spirit, which must be aware and engaged for spellcraft to work. So it's not surprising that many spells include the lighting, carving, or blowing out of a candle as part of the mixture. For example, a person might light a candle to ignite a love spell, or blow one out to dowse unwanted attention. Another individual might carve a candle with a symbol of his desire and let the candle burn down through the symbol to release the energy. Flashlights, lamps, matches, oil lamps, lighters, and tiki torches are all more contemporary options, but personally, I like the mystical ambience candlelight adds to any magical procedure. Because the modern options previously listed can't be carved, you have to get a little inventive with how you use them in the spell. Some examples include turning on a flashlight in lieu of using a wand to direct energy at the end of a spell; putting aromatic oils on a light bulb or in the oil lamp to release power; or igniting a torch at sunset to mark the sacred space in which you're working.

COLORS Color influences our conscious and subconscious actions and reactions. Consequently, it can strongly influence magical results. In spellcraft, components may be chosen for their color's mystical associations as shown in the chart below.

COLOR CORRESPONDENCES

Red: energy, love, power, bravery, vitality, fire
Orange: kindness, empathy, grace, outcomes
Yellow: inventiveness, mental keenness, psychism, air
Green: development, abundance, health
Blue: peace, thoughtfulness, happiness, water
Purple: spirituality, empathy, dedication

Black: banishing, rest, earth
White: reconciliation, Spirit, purification, safety

Exactly how the color is added into the spell is up to you. Put
accents of color in the working space via tablecloths, colored
lightbulbs, altar decorations, among others Use components that
are all the same color, such as mint, dill, and marjoram in a money
spell (all are green, and all accent prosperity). Dye a magic potion
using food coloring—use yellow to increase personal psychic
awareness. Wear a blue robe when working a spell for peace in a
relationship, red jewelry for increased energy, and so forth.

FLORA AND FAUNA   Trying to describe all the ways that animal
symbolism and plant parts can be used in spellcraft is a job suited
to an entire collection of books. Consequently, this is but a snap-
shot of a very complex and diversified component option.

Various plant parts are used in incense, in spell bags and boxes,
and in fetishes and charm creation. Plant parts may also be made
into magical beverages for libations or potions and into edibles
for internalizing the magic of a spell. I use these two options frequently because the symbolism of eating or drinking an item's
energy is potent on both a conscious and subconscious level.

Another alternative is using plants to symbolically decorate the
sacred space. For example, one might choose to place a potted
tulip in the northern quarter of a circle, lavender in the eastern
quarter, a red carnation in the southern quarter, and a violet in the
western quarter. Each of these plants elementally represents the
quarter in which they're placed.

Which part of a plant gets used and whether it is fresh or dried
depends much on the application in the spell—a dry plant being
easier to burn, for example. Seeds are great symbolically for "planting," "growing," and manifesting a specific type of energy. Dried or
fresh flower petals, fruit rinds, and other small parts can be scattered to the winds to carry magic on its way.

Animal symbolism in spellcraft is a little different. In times past
it was perfectly acceptable to use animal parts in magic, as the

creature represented a valuable sacrifice to the Divine. Today, Wiccans prefer more earth-friendly alternatives. Found feathers, snippets of hair, a stone carving, pictures, and visualizations of creatures have become substitutes for the real thing.

You see, a symbol is just as powerful as what it represents in the sacred space. So, where a dove's heart might have once been necessary for a love spell, now a feather or picture of the dove becomes a proxy. Where blood might have been added to a spell for power, now catsup or beet juice could be used. And, where whale fat might have been used in a spell for beauty, now people might listen to whale songs on tape instead, filling themselves with those lovely vibrations. The idea here is to honor the tradition and maintain a congruity of symbolism, while still living in reciprocity with nature.

KNOTS Knots are terrific spell components because you can bind energy within that is only released when the knot is undone. Knot magic is seen a lot in Arabic traditions, and in coastal communities who depend on fishing as a source of food and income. In the former tradition, a Corsair (sea person) might ask a wizard for a wind rope with knots, each of which could be released when the sails needed a boost. In the coastal tradition, the knots in the fishing nets could protect, provide, and bring fertility depending on their construction.

All types of knot spells exist in Wicca. Some people make spell braids, which are slowly undone over days, weeks, or even years to release magic toward its goal. Others use knots in clothing or jewelry to "bind" negativity and bad habits, and still other people may "tie" a type of energy to a location via a knot (like protecting a home using a knotted rug).

If you feel like being really creative, change the type of knot you use in your spell to mirror the goal. Four square knots, for example, might be best suited to holding elemental energy (earth-air-fire-water) that can be released when you need that power to energize a situation. A slip knot can be designed to temporarily hold a thought-form that you want to "disappear." And, a lover's knot is terrific for storing the special energy generated by relationships.

POPPETS AND FIGURINES   Poppets and figurines represent the person, animal, or place that they are fashioned to look like. Say a friend is sick and has asked you to cast a spell for her health. You might create a poppet out of a piece of her clothing and stuff it with healthful herbs (allspice, lemon balm, mint) to figuratively "fill" that individual with healing energy. Tend to the poppet as you might that person to extend your caring energy her way. Burn it or bury it afterward to dispel the sickness it has gathered.

For pets, a poppet allows you to attend to their needs when the creature will not. If the animal is grouchy from a stomach disturbance, for example, you could wash the stomach portion of his image with saltwater to spiritually purge that problem. Extending this idea a little bit, putting images of endangered species in a white cloth and adding a protective incantation daily might be one way to help safeguard those creatures from extinction. This type of magic can work for an image of the earth, too!

Alternatives provided in the commercial market include: stuffed animals, dolls, paintings (apply oils to these instead of herbs), stone carvings, clay replicas, models, earthenware or concrete statuary, likenesses on cups and goblets (which can be filled or emptied), or novelty candles.

WRITTEN OR SPOKEN WORDS   This element lies somewhere between being a component to spellcraft and being a technique. As a component, words may be written in designs on paper, spoken, or thought to empower the magic being created. The old charm of abracadabra provides us with one example, having been written so the word slowly vanishes, taking with it any sickness.

Thinking or verbalizing generally takes the form of an incantation that gives definition and details to the magic. When spoken out loud, the words add their vibrations to the energy. When recited inwardly, the thought-form carries power along with any visualization. This is why words in both spoken and written form can have a powerful effect on others, and personal thoughts can so strongly effect your outlook and actions.

Techniques

People are always writing me asking how to put together spell components for effective results. Once the ingredients of a magical recipe are gathered, the method of "cooking" the magic becomes important. For example, one person might find chanting or singing an effective technique for raising energy and releasing one's spell (see also Components, page 118). Other procedures to consider for personally created spells, or those you might use to adapt those given herein, follow.

NUMEROLOGY   In ancient times, people held that numbers had power even as words do. By using a symbolic number of components, repeating an incantation, or stirring a mixture a certain number of times, or by working on a specifically numbered date, it is possible to improve the power of a spell. If you'd like to add this technique into your spellcraft, use the following chart for numerical correspondences.

METAPHYSICAL ASSOCIATIONS OF NUMBERS

1: singlemindedness, individuality, wellness, sun/fire
2: duality, balance, harmony, agreement
3: trinity (both Divine and human), persistence, strength
4: foundations, the earth, attainment, purposefulness
5: magic, flexibility, psychic gifts, air
6: tenacity, protection, fulfillment
7: diversity, intuition, foresight, moon/water
8: leadership, changes, increasing energy
9: kindness, charity, Universal truth and justice

For a functional example, in preparing a love spell you might choose two components associated with relationships and repeat your incantation three times to represent unity of body–mind–spirit between the two of you.

Other ways to work numbers into your spellcraft include: anointing a date on a wall or desk calendar (manifestation); telephone numbers or zip codes (communication); using birth dates or license plate numbers (connections with others); choosing meaningful ATM codes (prosperity magic); and measurement amounts (increasing or decreasing energy). If any number is more than ten, you can reduce it to its component number by adding all figures together. For example, the date 2-21-1960 becomes

$$2 + 2 + 1 + 1 + 9 + 6 + 0 = 21 = 2 + 1 = 3$$

So this particular date would represent a 3 (tenacity). If you had an old 1960 calendar that you wanted to use as a component, pulling off that date and burning it with specially chosen herbs might be one way to activate more persistence in your life.

Physical Change

To make a spell more cohesive, consider ways to create changes in the components that mirror your goal. Use this list to help give you ideas.

Baking: gives the phrase "cooking something up" a whole new meaning. Use this to raise energy (bread is a good choice); warm up relationships; increase harmony (try stew); and bring things to slow, but steady, fruition.

Burning: warms the energy, releases power, acts as an offering or prayer, destroys the components (to symbolically rid you of something).

Burying: means that something is dead to you. But, the nice thing is that you can still plant something above it to create a positive from a negative.

Chilling: calms anger, helps you "chill out" with regard to a heated situation, or back off emotionally to get better perspective. Chilling also helps slow down progress when things are moving too quickly.

Composting: breaks down barriers and helps diverse energies (or people) work together for the greatest good. Also a figurative way of increasing fertility.

Crushing: defeats or overcomes a difficult problem or situation. Crushes undesired attention, and re-establishes personal control.

Cutting: separates or divides. A way of taking yourself out of a situation, or severing an unhealthy attachment to a person, place, habit, or thing.

Floating: sends your magical message through the earth's waters to their desired designation. Alternatively a symbolism of "rising above" the tide that surrounds.

Freezing: halts negativity, stops unwanted progressions, and reflects back any bad intentions to their source.

Microwaving: speeds up the manifestation process.

Melting: warms up a chilly disposition, loosens up blockage, improves the figurative "flow" of energy.

Molding: shapes your magic into the form it's meant to have upon completion, which improves the accuracy and speed of manifestation. Also a way of helping you "fit into" a difficult pair of shoes by sculpting things differently.

Planting: helps energy grow and blossom. Alternatively, a way of grounding yourself or rooting a type of magic to one specific region.

Scattering: releases the energy to the winds, birds, animals, among others, to carry it where it's most needed. Alternatively a way of releasing something you no longer need.

Washing: cleanses and purifies the energy. Alternatively a way of washing away habits, sickness, unproductive thought-forms, and societal "dirt."

As you can see, what happens to the components during a spell should make sense considering the spell's purpose. For example, to draw love, one would not use scissors unless you needed to separate yourself from some unwanted affections first. Or, to improve the speed with which a spell manifests, I wouldn't suggest freezing the components unless those components represent an obstacle or source of curtailment to overcome.

Elemental, Directional, or Astrological Correspondences

When creating a spell to increase personal intuition, one might choose components that all have lunar associations. Metaphysical books on herbs and stones usually list their planetary and elemental correspondence for your reference. If you're uncertain what these correspondences mean, use the following chart.

ELEMENT/DIRECTION

East/Air: mental ability, communication, whimsy, hope, new beginnings, the winds of change

South/Fire: purification, energy, passion, intensity, willpower, drive, bravery, vitality

West/Water: health, emotions, kindness, restitution, kinship, dream work, psychic empowerment, "flow"

North/Earth: rest, peace, progress, fertility, money, foundations, earth healing, standing one's ground

PLANETARY

Sun: mental keenness, leadership, personal energy and power, legalities, health, the body, clarification

Moon: intuition, emotions, restfulness, fertility, kindness, inner peace, psychism, the spiritual nature

Mercury: communication, fortune-telling, speech, learning, sagacity, adventure, advancement

Venus: devotion, relationships, love, passion, beauty, kinship, thoughfulness, reconciliation

Earth: grounding, security, growth, home, reason, stability, putting down roots

Mars: strength, bravery, sexuality, banishing, protection, effective confrontation

Jupiter: faith, spiritual quests, contemplation, trance work, religious insight

Saturn: focus, safety, cleansing, good fortune, grounding, serendipity

Note that Uranus, Neptune, and Pluto are not included in this list. They were not known to the ancient magicians. Looking to the future, these planets will probably be given metaphysical associations correlated to their names, such as Uranus being associated with celestial energy as Uranus comes from *Urania* in Greek, meaning "heavenly one." She was the Muse of astronomy. Neptune might get aligned with sea-dwelling stones and plants, being the name of the Roman God of the Ocean, and Pluto could be associated with root crops and death, as Pluto is another name for Hades, the god of the underworld.

Visualization

This is an important technique in many magical workings, not just spellcraft. Visualization equates to will-driven imagining (see also chapter 3). By opening our spiritual eyes, we give form and dimension to the magic's goal, which brings improved results.

To understand how this works, think about water. Outside of a container it simply breaks apart and disperses to who knows where. Once put into a cup, bowl, or ice cube tray, however, it takes on a recognizable shape. Magical energy is like water. Without form and direction it simply disperses back to the Source. Visualizations provide that much needed direction and shape for magical energy to become a functional pattern mirroring your goal.

Incantation

The words spoken to energize a spell are very important. They, like visualization, add another dimension to your magic through the vibrations and meanings of the words. Incantations also affect you.

Think of viewing a movie without sound. You can guess what people are saying, and what's going on, but you won't be *sure* unless you're a very good lip-reader! In magic, the visualization acts like a "soundtrack" for Sacred Powers. It communicates exactly what you hope to achieve so that the energy you create can be directed for the greatest good. The incantation also reiterates your intentions to your own mind, thereby reinforcing your resolve and focus.

In some cases, the end of an incantation indicates the completion of the spell's procedure(s). When this occurs the volume of the incantation often rises to a pinnacle to build power like inflating a balloon with energy. Silence then falls abruptly, cutting the energy balloon free to go on its way.

Most of the incantations in this chapter rhyme or have a rhythmic pattern. I generally recommend using rhyme and meter in your personal incantations or adaptations. This makes them easier to remember, giving you more freedom to focus on the energy they create.

Special Timing

A chart of astrological times for creating amulets and charms is given in chapter 4. This chart can also be used in determining when to cast a specific spell. The ancient mages trusted the Celestial time clock tremendously as an energizer for magic. And while modern schedules don't always allow for such details, symbolic timing can be very helpful.

The more the particulars of a spell make sense to us, the better the results are bound to be. For example, cast a spell to banish a bad habit on New Year's, when many other people are resolving to do likewise. Cast spells for health, luck, and happiness on your birthday. Or, go with more traditional approaches and wait for a waxing to full moon to enact a spell for personal growth and maturity.

While I tend to believe that any time is the "right" time for magic, and that personal need doesn't always wait for perfect astrological conjunctions, the benefits to choosing a time for a spell shouldn't be underestimated. The process of deciding helps you think more clearly about your goals and what they mean to you. It also puts you in touch with ancient magical traditions and allows you to reclaim that legacy for future generations.

Divine Guidance

This is a method many people use to steer their magic more effectively and carefully. If you have a specific God or Goddess that you follow, or if you simply call on the Great Spirit, this ancient persona is the energy core for magic. Trusting that such a power must be far wiser than myself, I prefer to leave the directional supervision of magical energy in the hands of the Sacred.

If you would like to do likewise, you can use the universal clause that's included in many Wiccan spells and rituals: "for the greatest good, and it harm none." By adding this onto the end of a spell, you release your magical energy to the Divine, acknowledging the fact that you can't foresee all the potential outcomes for that magical working. The Divine, however, has the vantage point that we do not and can guide the energy for the most beneficial outcome. This may change the anticipated results of a spell in unexpected and sometimes humorous ways, but the results will always be "for the greatest good."

Finally, don't forget the methods that your own body can help you enact. Close your eyes to focus your resolve. Dance or chant to raise power. Point or extend a wand to direct power. Sit down to ground out energy. Reach out to welcome the magical attributes generated by your spell into your spirit. You are always the most important element and tool in your magic.

Keys to Success

> Perhaps everyone can learn to cast spells, just as nearly everyone can learn to sing, but to shatter a wine glass is quite another matter.
>
> —J. Finley Hurley

Magic is an art, meaning that preparation, practice, and persistence are the three primary keys to success. One will not become adept at spellcraft overnight. Its an ongoing process of experimentation to find what approaches work best for you. The techniques presented in this book can be mixed and matched in numerous ways, but exactly which way proves successful for each individual varies. You are a unique spiritual being whose magical expressions should likewise be unique.

Beyond the element of practice, a respectful attitude that acknowledges and appreciates the sacredness of all things is very important. Having this mindset accomplishes two things. First, a person who honors himself, nature, and others, will rarely abuse magical knowledge. Second, this same individual will be able to see the magical potential in everything, from the smallest grain of sand to the farthest star, and most importantly within his or her own heart.

TEN KEYS TO SUCCESSFUL SPELLCRAFT

1. Work with the right attitude and intention.
2. Be responsible to yourself and others.
3. Understand and trust the process.
4. Personalize the spell's "recipe," but keep it simple.
5. Follow natural patterns; go with the flow.
6. Cleanse, bless, and consecrate the spell's ingredients.
7. Focus on your goal throughout the process.
8. Ask for Divine guidance, if desired.
9. Release the magic.
10. Reinforce the magic.

Next in successful spellcraft comes the rule of culpability. You are responsible for the results of any magic you raise and direct. Whatever you send out will return to you threefold. It seems only prudent, then, to carefully and thoughtfully design spells so they do not manipulate another's free will, and so they result in the most positive energy possible. In the long run, this approach benefits not only you, but everyone your life touches.

Fourth, don't just pick up a spell book and start casting spells randomly. Returning to point three, this is very irresponsible, especially if there's any part of the spell to which you don't relate or about which you feel uncomfortable. Always take the time to understand the process you're using, and trust in it before proceeding.

Fifth, personalize prefabricated spells or make your own from scratch, but keep things as simple as possible. While medieval spell books indicate odd or unsavory components, mysterious words, and highly detailed procedures for each spell given, one must regard these accounts cautiously. They were often written by those wishing to undermine mystical traditions in the eyes of a very superstitious public. In other instances, mages wrote their notes like a cryptography, neatly keeping the *real* magical procedure out of the hands of novices. So, the Bard's "eye of newt" may have actually been a code for something as simple as a bean or bit of chicken!

We live in a world where "fancier" often equates with "better"—but that's not necessarily the case in Wicca. Keeping a spell uncomplicated does not negatively effect its potency. In fact, the simpler a spell is, and the more meaning it holds for you, the better the results are likely to be! True to the tradition of folk magic, the homegrown approach frees your mind and spirit to focus wholly on the task of generating, releasing, and directing energy.

Sixth, don't swim upstream. Everything in the world follows patterns and cycles. Whenever possible, construct your spells so they mirror those patterns. For example, when planting a seed component so love grows in your life, don't put the seed in the microwave to "speed up" the process. From a purely scientific vantage point, the radiation isn't good for the seed, so it's not good for your magic. From a spiritual perspective, some things can't be rushed if they're going to last. Relationships definitely fall into that category.

Seventh, always use clean tools and components in your spell-craft. Objects and items can pick up residual energy just from sitting in one spot for a few minutes. The likelihood that the energy an object or item absorbs is synchronous with your magical goal is slim. So, take a minute and cleanse (see chapter 4) the ingredients of your spell, including yourself. Take a quick shower or herbal bath, or just dab yourself with some flower water to adjust auric energy into balance with your magical goals.

Once the components are clean, you may wish to bless and consecrate them. Blessing invokes Divine favor and assistance. Consecration sets the components apart for a specific function in the spell. The easiest way to bless and consecrate is by holding the items in hand, or holding your hands over them, and saying a brief prayer while visualizing the white light of spirit filling the components.

Eighth, throughout the casting of the spell, make sure you maintain focus. Take any steps necessary so you don't get interrupted. Shape the central idea and intention of the magic in your mind, be tenacious, build the energy through word and deed. Keep this concentration level until the spell is completed. During this deeply thoughtful time, ask for Divine guidance, if desired. Do this with words that are comfortable to you, and in a manner suited to your Path.

Next, release the spell. All the energy in the world won't do much good unless it reaches its mark. When you let the energy go, release your expectations with it. Trust that the magic will do what it should *somehow*, but also know that the outcome might not be what you envisioned. For example, a person working magic for advancement at work might be given that opportunity by being offered extra hours or projects instead of the hoped promotion.

Last, but not least, reinforce the magic with both metaphysical and mundane efforts. Repeat the spell as often as you wish until it manifests, and do everything possible in your daily life to help that manifestation process along. If you're casting spells for a better job, for example, bless your résumés with a prosperous aromatic, look through the paper every week, and contact employment agencies right after finishing the spell. In magic, and in life, the Gods truly help those who are willing to help themselves.

Seasonal Spells

> Whosoever readeth spells daily over himself, he is whole upon the earth.
>
> —*Egyptian Book of the Dead*

Spring

Spring is the season for new beginnings and renewed hope. It is also associated with the element air, so this spell combines wind with the desire for an upbeat outlook for magic that draws heartening energy to you.

Go outside at dawn with a handful of lavender flowers and freshly picked morning glories. As the sun first shines over the horizon, scatter these to the wind moving clockwise, saying:

> *Happiness without, hope within*
> *I give this joy to the winds.*
> *As these petals fly free,*
> *Bring happiness back to me.*

Summer

Summer is a fire season, and one filled with social activity. This spell releases energy by fire to improve personal physical energy for the demands of the season.

Go outside at noon on a day when the sun is bright in the sky. Have a barbecue grill or other fire source lit and a handful of bay leaves and red carnation petals. Hold these in your hands, visualizing the fire of the sun and the fire in front of you as filling your

being until you nearly burst with energy. Then, release the bay
and carnation to the flames saying:

> *As carnations and bay begin to ignite*
> *So my magic takes to flight.*
> *The flames release energy*
> *So the power grows in me!*

Fall

Fall is associated with the element water and is characterized by
abundance. This spell releases energy through water to improve
figurative or literal prosperity in any area of your life.

To begin, you'll need a flowing water source. A natural one's
best, but a hose will do. You'll also need a bundle of dry
chamomile (empty out a tea bag). Go to the water source in the
late afternoon. Stand in such a way that the water source flows
toward you, then reach out as far as you can and sprinkle the
chamomile on the water upstream saying:

> *Abundance to me, Abundance flow free*
> *Today I claim prosperity.*

If you wish to, gather a little of the chamomile from the water and
dry it to carry as a charm.

Winter

Winter is aligned with the element earth and is characterized by
frugality. This spell combines soil with the energy of conservation
to improve prudence.

Begin with a coin, some brown wrapping paper, and a patch of
earth. Wrap the coin in the paper, symbolically preserving it, as
you say:

> *A coin wrapped, a coin conserved*
> *Help me keep resources preserved!*

Plant the coin and paper in the soil near your home so that frugal energy comes to you. Come spring, dig up the coin and carry it as an amulet that preserves finances.

Thematic Spells

Enchant me with your spells of art, and draw me homeward to your heart.

—Lionel Johnson

These spells are designed to meet common human needs and desires that are part of our makeup, and therefore not likely to disappear soon. We all wish for good companions, good health, a little extra money. Good magical formulas can bring these things to us, and help with a lot of everyday situations.

Flexibility

As we move into the future, I feel one thing we're going to need in abundance is flexibility. This not only means adapting our magic, but our ways of thinking and be-ing. This spell is designed to improve personal adaptive ability.

Begin with seven pieces of apple, a pinch of rosemary, a yellow cloth, and a white ribbon. On the first night of a full moon at midnight (the witching hour), place the rosemary in the cloth, and each apple slice one at a time saying:

One, the spell has just begun; two, flexibility clear and true;
Three, adjustment comes to me; four within the power to store;
Five, the spell comes alive; six, the magic I now affix;
Seven components neatly wrapped; grant me the power to adapt.

Secure the top of the bundle with the ribbon (which is flexible). Burn, bury, or scatter the bundle's contents when you want the magic to manifest.

Friendship

Friends are among the most treasured things in life. Those who stay with us through good times and bad, long into the future, are also those who are often part of a karmic group. This group learns and grows together spiritually. This spell is designed to draw friends with whom you can interact on this level for many years to come.

For this spell you'll need a pink candle with the word *friendship* carved on it and a handful of dried lemon peel. If possible work when the moon is in Aquarius. Place the candle in a window where you live. Light it, thinking about all the qualities you would enjoy in a friend (common interests, adventurous spirit, or whatever). Now, go outside and sprinkle the walk up to your home (or apartment building) with the dried lemon saying:

> *Come to me, friends who will be true and kind*
> *Come to me, to share, learn, and grow together*
> *Come to me.*

Repeat this incantation until you've used up all but one pinch of the lemon. Keep this remainder with you to help draw potential friends your way.

Gossip

I personally hate gossip. It is a very harmful, self-serving tendency that can destroy a person's life. When you discover that someone (or a group) is spreading inaccurate or malicious gossip about you, use this spell.

Begin with a poppet shaped like a person (this can represent one person or a group mind). Fill the poppet with dried orange, cloves, and dry grass. Stitch it shut. Sew Xs over the poppet's mouth. With each X you sew, say:

> *Only truth may escape your lips*
> *Silence the lies; silence the negativity*
> *By my will, all hearsay be still.*

Keep this in a safe place. If the problem doesn't show signs of improvement within two weeks, burn the poppet to cleanse away negative energy and disperse it to the winds.

Health

The New Age has brought a renewed focus on physical health as being strongly intertwined with mental and spiritual well-being. This spell is designed to safeguard all aspects of one's health.

Begin with a blend of orange juice and apple juice to which you add a drop of mint extract (the amount is less important than the symbolism). Put this in a clear glass and hold it up to the sunlight saying:

> *Healthy body, healthy mind*
> *Healthy spirit, here the magic I bind.*
> *Chase all maladies neatly away.*
> *Bring renewed wholeness starting today.*

Drink the juice to internalize the magic.

Love

Love stretches the range of human interactions by asking us to do and be the very best person we can be. For some people, however, it's very hard to open themselves to love because of past failures. For others, it's hard to accept love because they do not love themselves. This spell is designed to overcome past pains, instill self-appreciation, and open the path for giving and receiving love.

Enact this spell on a Friday, the day traditionally beneficial to relationships (including the way you relate to yourself). Have a bowl of rose petals ready and a small mint candy. Hold the candy in both hands, visualizing it filled with a pinkish-white light saying:

> *Healing within, let it begin*
> *Self-love grow where this sweetness goes.*

Eat the mint then take the rose petals in hand. Visualize these filled with a vibrant red light then sprinkle them around yourself in a clockwise circle outdoors. As you turn repeat the phrase:

> *Petals be free, love return to me.*

Let the winds carry the petals to potential mates.

Luck

Serendipity makes life interesting and a lot more fun. Yet, there seems to be times when a little luck is nowhere to be found. When those occasions come up, try this spell.

If possible, spells for luck are best cast during the spring, which has upbeat, hopeful energy. Take a personally lucky number of quarters and bless them saying:

> *Where good fortune is given, some will return.*
> *In these coins, the magic burns.*
> *Luck be free; luck to me.*

Keep the quarters with you. When you see a parking meter about to expire, put one of the coins in it and repeat your incantation. This neatly blesses another person and releases the power of your magic.

Money

As much as we might wish for a future where money won't matter, I don't see that happening anytime soon. When you find your financial situation spoiling spiritual pursuits or hindering joy, try making this prosperity incense.

Begin with equal amounts of any four of the following herbs (four is the number of earthly matters): basil, cinnamon, ginger, mint, nutmeg, orange. Blend this with an equal portion of any powdered or slivered wood, like cedar, sandlewood, or pine. This helps the mixture burn readily. Whenever you need a little extra cash, put a pinch of this on a safe fire source saying:

> *Through the winds, through the flame*
> *Prosperity, I claim!*
> *By this smoke my wish is free*
> *Bring prosperity to me.*

Keep the remaining incense in a dark, airtight container until you need it again. This usually retains a good aroma for a year.

Opportunity

Waiting for your ship to come in? Tired of knocking on brick walls that never give way? This spell is designed to create opportunities in your life. Once these doors open, it's up to you to step through them.

For this spell you'll need a handful of daisy petals and an open window, preferably one that faces east (beginnings). Stand by the window at sunrise holding the petals in hand. Visualize the petals being filled with green and gold light until they feel almost warm in your palm. Then open the window and release the petals saying:

> *Through this window I open the way*
> *For more opportunities starting today!*

To further energize the magic, repeat the spell every day for one full week—then just keep your eyes and ears open!

Psychism

We are living in an era when even science recognizes that there's more to the human mind than we understand. In the future I believe our psychic abilities will become more important and necessary to overall improvements in the human condition. This spell is designed to augment your personal psychic gifts and awareness.

During the night of a full moon take a large bay leaf and trace the image of an eye upon it. Crush the bay leaf in your hands to release the energy saying:

> *Mystic awareness, Spiritual light*
> *Let me see with inner sight*
> *As this magic takes to flight.*

When you say the word "flight" toss the crushed bay out into the air so the energy begins manifesting.

Children's Spells

Where are you now? Who lies beneath your spell?

—Lawrence Hope

As with other types of magic, children's spells need to be simple but also colorful and meaningful. Children relate to symbols and rhyme very well (that's why we have nursery rhymes), meaning, their capacity to work effective spells is fairly natural. The adult's role here is to ensure that the magical procedure is safe and that the child understands what he or she is doing.

Promises

It's often hard for children to keep promises because they simply forget that they have made them. When a child finds that she is constantly getting into trouble because of this, she can try this spell to assist herself.

If possible, have the child cast this spell on a Thursday to accentuate commitment. Fill a small container with jelly beans (in mystical tradition, beans improve our ability to judge situations wisely), and bless the container by saying:

> *Help me do as I say, let this magic start today.*
> *A promise kept, a promise made*
> *Let my promises never fade.*

The child can then eat one or two jelly beans daily to improve her dedication to a promise.

Relaxation

With my own children, the concept of downtime seems to be almost nonexistent. Yet I believe teaching children to relax is important so they also learn self-control. This little spell is designed to improve a child's ability to calm down.

For the spell you'll need a white or blue airtight container and seven almonds or seven pieces of sugar-free blueberry-flavored gum. Have the child put these in the container by the light of a waxing moon saying:

> *When taken within*
> *Calm will begin.*
> *Like an anchor of tranquility*
> *Self-control grows in me.*

She can carry this container with her, eating one of the candies and reciting the incantation whenever she needs a more peaceful demeanor. Refill and recharge as desired.

Safety

I don't think there are parents in the world who don't worry about their children's safety. Our society has become a dangerous place for young ones, meaning a little magical protection certainly won't hurt.

To begin this safety spell, you'll need one cup of baking soda and one teaspoon each of dried mint (finely chopped) and powdered clove. Have the child mix these together on a bright, sunny day, stirring clockwise as he or she says:

> *Light without, light within*
> *Let this magic spell begin.*
> *Keep me guarded well, safe to be*
> *Knowing the Light walks with me.*

Whenever you or the child is concerned about peers or other situations, sprinkle this mixture in her shoes before she leaves for school or play.

Wishes

Of all childhood pastimes, wishing is one that most people remember fondly. The enchanting thing is that many traditional wishes are actually folk spells. Think of wishing on the first star appearing. The accompanying rhyme is actually an incantation! Tossing coins into wells with wishes can also become a magical procedure just by adding a verbal component or visualization. This particular spell combines the coin with starlight for easy recognition by the child.

Find any silver-colored coin with the child's birth year on it. Have him take it out at dusk and wait for the first star to appear. As it does, have him hold the coin up to the starlight saying:

> *Catch the starlight in this coin so bright*
> *I'll get the wish I wish tonight.*
> *Within this coin my wish is carried*
> *The magic will grow when it's buried.*

Have the child put the coin into an area of rich soil where it will remain undisturbed so the spell can grow to manifestation.

Earth-Healing Spells

> Without haste, without rest, bind the motto to thy breast!
> Bear it with thee as a spell; storm or sunshine guard it
> well.
>
> —Goethe

Because the theme of this magic is spreading positive energy throughout the globe, I've designed these spells with components that can be scattered by the wind, floated on water, burned as incense, or grown in the ground. Symbolically, these actions bear the energy you create to where it can do the most good. If you change the base components, please make sure anything you use is not harmful to animals or the planet (that would defeat the magic's purpose).

Earth Awareness

Living in reciprocity with nature and remaining aware of its needs is a function of the conscious mind...consciously changing the way we act and live so as to be more "earth friendly."

For this spell you will need a package of either celery seed or rosemary seed and a place where you can plant these. The location doesn't matter as long as the earth is rich, and you can periodically tend them. Leave the seed pack in the sunlight for a while to absorb its energies. Then take the seeds to the planting location, putting them lovingly in the soil as you mentally or verbally use an incantation like this one:

> *Seeds of awareness, root in us,*
> *Seeds of perception, grow in us,*
> *Seeds of understanding, blossom in us.*

Each time you go to this spot, recite the incantation again and tend the seedlings so the magic grows.

Gaia's Body

Each day, somewhere in the world, rain falls to nourish the land. No matter what you place in water, or where, it will eventually return to serve Gaia's body, which is why a water source is used in this spell.

Begin with some dried bay leaves and dry black tea. Crush the bay leaves and mix them thoroughly with the tea, stirring clockwise saying:

> *Round and round, wholeness abounds*
> *Health within, let the magic begin.*

Take this mixture to any source of water and release the herbs into it. They will bear your healing magic when that water returns to the earth.

Gaia's Mind

Today and tomorrow one of the things that the human mind needs is an improved understanding of its place in the greater Universal mind, or collective unconscious. This spell is designed to heighten that comprehension.

You'll need some mustard seed (which represents faith and mental keenness) and some thyme (for psychic awareness). Stand facing west (the area of intuition) and say:

> *Wind of intuition take this thyme*
> *Bring spiritual awareness to mankind.*

Release the thyme. Then turn to face east (the region of hope) and say:

> *Wind of new beginnings take this seed*
> *The human mind and heart, with hope, is freed!*

Release the mustard to the wind. Visualize your energy being carried out in all directions from that place like a healing balm.

Gaia's Spirit

Spirit is connected strongly with the element of fire, as the burning Source within our heart. So this spell uses fire to consume the components and send their message directly to the God/dess's ear.

Begin by gathering together some violet petals and shards of sandalwood (both accentuate matters of the spirit). Also, find a safe fire source in which to burn them. Ignite the fire source and visualize the flames reaching up to the heavens. Slowly sprinkle on your components saying:

> *Let the Spirit within us burn brightly,*
> *Let it light the night and guide our way*
> *To a better future and a peaceful today.*

Take the fire source with the herbs burning in it and walk in a clockwise circle repeating the incantation at all four directional points so the aroma of magic spreads to the four corners of creation.

New Millennium Spells

> At the beginning of the scientific revolution, magic and the new science were allies.... It is time for magic and science to be allies again.
>
> —Michael Edwards

Humankind's ability to grow and adapt is nearly limitless. We have gone from harnessing fire to traveling among the stars in a very short time. With such rapid expansion we find ourselves amid a technological explosion, often at nature's expense. But not all technology is anthetical to Wiccan beliefs—in fact, some of it can be used to further our magic through its symbolism.

For example, say there's a specific characteristic you're trying to develop. Why not name a personal journal file on your computer after that attribute? That way each time you open the file, you are also figuratively "opening" positive energy and "retrieving" it into your life! These spells illustrate other ways to creatively blend modern means with ancient powers.

Adaptation

While humans seem to be a fairly adaptable lot, we are also creatures of habit, meaning that change often comes with a lot of labor pains. To help prepare yourself for future transitions, begin today with this adaptation spell that augments flexibily.

If possible perform this spell at midnight, noon, dusk, or dawn (all of which emphasize transition). The only component you'll need is a sturdy balloon. Go outside on a day when an easterly wind is blowing (to accent modification) and place the balloon over your index finger. Stretch and release tension on it seven times with your other hand (for completion), while focusing on your intention and saying:

> *Stretch and bend, bend and change*
> *Magic is to bend and change.*
> *Like this token let me be*
> *Filled with flexibility.*

Put this on a keychain or other regularly carried item. If the balloon ever breaks, just get a new one and do the spell again. If you need immediate help, inflate the balloon to increase energy.

Communication

Our society has become increasingly mobile. Consequently, maintaining good lines of communication is all the more important. Excellent components to emphasize this goal are portable phones, cell phones, or CB radios. Take your choice of the three for this spell.

Get your chosen component along with a piece of paper, a yellow marker, and a piece of clear tape. On the paper inscribe an image of *raido*, the rune of communication (this looks like an R except the round edge is triangular). Focus on your intention to listen, and really hear, the communications that come to you. Adhere the paper to the handset of the main component saying:

> *Open the way, that I may hear*
> *Open the way, that I may listen*
> *Open the way, that I may speak clearly*
> *Open the way to understanding.*

If the tape ever begins wearing off, or the paper underneath it yellows, put a new symbol on your phone or radio. Any time you want to communicate with a specific person, touch the image, visualize their face, and repeat the incantation. Unless it's a very distant someone, you should hear from her within a week's time.

Harmony

Harmony comes when people with various talents come together with a common cause. A great way to accent this kind of energy is by making a drinkable spell using a food processor to blend unity from diversity.

Begin with apple juice (for wisdom and love), a drop of lemon (for abiding friendship), and a few drops of warm catnip tea (for happiness). Mix these together on a low setting saying:

> *Round and round*
> *The magic's bound*
> *Harmony, unity, and accord*
> *When from this pitcher poured.*

Pour this into a cup garnished with a mint leaf (peace and harmony). By having everyone drink from one common glass, you strengthen the symbolism of unified thought and action.

Protection

Ever just want to turn off the problems in your life, even for just a moment or two? Why not freeze the negative energy? Take a piece of paper on which you've written the source of your problems. Put this in an ice cube tray and fill it with slightly soapy water. As you place the tray in the freezer say:

> *Away from me, all negativity*
> *Halted in your path, washed away by this bath,*
> *Be frozen within as this spell begins.*

Once the cube is frozen solid, extract it and put it in the back of the freezer where it will remain undisturbed.

Quick Cash

I can think of at least a hundred times when I needed just five or ten dollars to get by. When you face something similar, try this spell. You'll need an old bank card (one that you don't need any-more) and a microwave (for speeding things up).

For safety reasons, put the old card in some cold water then place it on the microwave tray. Set the timer for nine seconds (nine is a very magical number as it is three threes). After you set the timer, repeat the following:

> *Money I claim, money quickly I need*
> *By my will this spell is freed.*

Let the card cool, then carry it with you until the spell manifests (usually within one week). Afterward, keep it for other money spells or discard it (it will not usually work in the ATM after this procedure).

Modern approaches to spellcraft offer us the chance to make our magic meaningful in the new millennium, and practical, consider-ing the transitions that the future will likely bring. Additionally, by approaching our spellcraft with a creative, future-looking eye, we make it more immediately serviceable for future generations.

6

Rituals and Invocations

Inward religion without the outward show of it is like a tree without fruit, useless; and the outward show of religion without inward sincerity is like a tree without heart, lifeless.

—Ralph Venning

The body is a temple for the soul. Within this sacred space of self, Wiccans believe that life can become a ritual and an act of worship. It all comes down to the attitude with which one approaches each moment of living. But there are times when we want something more formalized—times when we want to honor the Sacred in a ceremony, celebrate a special occasion metaphysically, or just find a moment's peace in a personally created sanctuary. Ritual provides one possible mechanism for these goals.

Before the idea of ritual scares you off, realize that many things you do are already ritualistic. By definition, a ritual is simply *any* regularly observed routine. In the everyday scheme of things, rituals are simply habits and patterns that we follow to give life

coherence, continuity, and familiarity. Some we create for ourselves, and some we get by way of tradition. For example, I am
religious about my morning ritual—a cup of coffee, light on the
cream, before starting to write. The ritual of meticulously deco-
rating my Yule tree comes from my dad, who wouldn't hear of
having one ornament out of place.

In Wicca, ritual has similar connotations. Each ritual follows a
pattern that has a goal, be it personal, seasonal, or whatever. Those
rituals that prove successful and fulfilling become traditions to
individuals or entire groups. Wiccan ritual has one dimension that
daily rituals do not, however—that of a religious element.

Before a Wiccan ritual begins, a practitioner invokes Divine or
devic powers (called Quarters) for energy and protection. This
invocation creates a sacred space within which magical energy will
be built, directed, and released through a scripted combination of
prayers, spells, invocations, meditations, and other symbolic, meaningful actions. Thus, rituals "wrap up" the progression we've built
with a functional metaphysical construct. Inside this construct, all
other steps to successfully bringing magic into the future—developing insight, the right attitude, improved awareness, increased
flexibility, and a creative blueprint—work smoothly and effectively.

The Ritual Process

In rituals and faith excel.

—George W. Bungay

Every ritual will be slightly different depending on its purpose,
the people involved, and the Wiccan tradition represented. Generally speaking, Wiccans use ritual to celebrate the seasons, mark
personal transformations, help with specific needs, and to honor
Divine personas. Really, anything for which you might cast a spell
could also be an occasion for a ritual, if time permits.

Rituals vary from spells in that they are longer, have more
detailed content, take place in a specially created sacred space, and

often include libations or offerings. But let's take this one step at a time. First come the pre-ritual preparations, like making an outline of the ritual's progression (with any personally desired changes). In writing a ritual, or looking over a traditional one given you, make sure you're comfortable with the movements, words, and activities, and that they make sense considering the ritual's goal and theme. Many books include sample rituals, but not all of these will suit your Path or personal vision. Thus, just as with spells, you're going to want to tweak portions of the ritual until they really "sing" the song in your soul.

RITUAL PROCESS

1. Review or create the ritual's script.
2. Make any personal changes desired.
3. Gather necessary props, components, costumes.
4. Consider a location for the ritual.
5. Gather people who want to participate.
6. Prepare the area for the ritual.
7. Create sacred space.
8. Raise and direct energy by using the script.
9. Allow for intuitive changes.
10. Release energy and close the circle.
11. Ground yourself.
12. Share and integrate the ritual's effects.
13. Make notes of everyone's experiences.

If you're working with a group, try to adjust the script so it gives interested members a role in the proceedings. In group dynamics, energy increases in proportion to the amount of participation. It also makes people feel needed and wanted—two emotions that in themselves can generate power through conviction and self assurance—in the sacred space.

Second, find appropriate decorations, props, and costumes so that every part of the ritual works together harmoniously with the theme. For example, during a winter celebration, cover the altar in white with cotton that has silver glitter sprinkled on top so it looks like snow. Have everyone dress in white and wear snowflake masks. Even if you're in California, the effect is very wintery and sets the ritual scene beautifully.

Third, determine the ritual's location. If you're working alone it's easy to hold a ritual in nearly any room of your home. Then again, some rituals (like for finding a familiar, or connecting with nature) are more suited to outdoor locations if feasible. Also, please bear in mind safety and accessibility in your ritual's locations. If, for example, you have participants with physical limitations, a long hike in the woods isn't reasonable.

Fourth, gather the participants. It is not necessary to work ritual in a group; in fact many people prefer working alone. Nonetheless, group work increases the overall energy you'll be able to create. It also has other benefits, like the chance to share with, and learn from, like-minded folk.

After the pre-ritual preparations are completed and the date for the ritual arrives, it is time to look seriously at your planned ritual space. If you're working outside, clear away any debris that might trip someone, use glow-in-the-dark tape on small trees that might not be seen in the dark, and rope off any patches of poison ivy and oak. Also, take proper fire precautions like digging trenches around the ritual fire, having a fire extinguisher on hand, allowing for adequate space between the participants and the fire, and using enclosed candles (lantern style) on the altar.

If you're working indoors, use a room with adequate space for all participants. Move furniture and breakables away from the circle's perimeter (this is very important if you plan to dance). Keep any fire sources far away from curtains and other flammable objects. Make provisions for any member with special physical needs (like keeping a chair handy for a pregnant woman).

All this effort sounds very nonmagical, but the rules of safety first and common courtesy don't go out the window just because you're working magic. A little forethought goes a long way toward making a successful, satisfying ritual. If anything, we should be more mindful so that the experience isn't hindered by injury or other mishaps.

Next comes the step of creating sacred space. Think of this like a sphere of energy that holds the energy you create in place until released, and keeps out any unwanted influences. When one is working with spiritual forces there is always a chance that some unsavory element might stray in your direction. The sacred space is designed to reflect away those elements.

Sacred space also marks a line between world and "not world." This region is regarded as being outside of time, which is why you'll notice many Wiccans do not wear watches to a ritual. It is also a magical realm where the possibilities are as endless as one's faith will allow. Once we enter this sphere, a sincere effort is made to leave the mundane world behind and focus wholly on the Sacred and our purpose.

The way of creating sacred space seems to be fairly universal but for wording and starting points. A practitioner moves around the space clockwise, stopping at the directional points and the center. As she goes, she visualizes a circle of light, invokes the powers that reside at those points, and welcomes the respective presences. Once in a while, the Quarters are called counterclockwise, but this is usually reserved for banishings.

Depending on the type of ritual, calling the Quarters is either part of the observance or is done just prior to it. For example, say someone is planning a wedding that many non-Wiccan family members will be attending. In this instance, the Quarters might be set in place beforehand so guests don't feel uncomfortable or misunderstand the proceedings.

Once sacred space has been established, the activities begin. These can include, but are not limited to, lighting special candles, burning incense, dancing, singing, chanting, prayers, meditations, visualizations, pathworking, ritual theater, spells, and sharing of a cup or edibles. Each activity is designed specifically to improve the symbolic effect of the ritual on the participant(s), and build energy that accentuates the ritual's goal or theme.

Toward the end of the ritual the energy created will be released or internalized by the participant(s). For example, a ritual designed for earth healing might end with the participants placing their hands into the soil and channeling all the energy they created to the planet. A ritual designed to improve a participant's health might end with all those gathered turning one palm toward that person to direct healthful energy where it's needed. A ritual designed to increase psychic awareness in the attendees might end with a quiet visualization where the participants draw the energy into themselves in the form of light that streams into the Third Eye (the psychic chakra).

At this point, most Wiccans close the circle. This is done by dismissing the Quarters and thanking the Powers for their help and protection. Usually the dismissal is similar to the invocation, but done in reverse order. Dismissal brings closure to the ritual and prepares the participants to return to mundane modes of thought and communication.

Following the dismissal, it's important that people take time to ground themselves. Magical workings can create a heady feeling and leave people in a nearly dreamlike state. So, sitting down and eating something crunchy (like raw vegetables) is suggested. This will help get your feet back on the ground. For safety reasons, I recommend at least fifteen minutes of adjustment time before anyone considers driving.

During this free time, share and integrate the ritual experience. Write about the ritual in a journal or discuss it. What about the ritual felt right? What did you like the best? Did anything affect you profoundly? If so, how? Note all these things and read them over later for more understanding. Also, read over the notes anytime you're thinking about doing this same ritual again so you can fine-tune it. If you keep this record diligently, you'll eventually have an entire book of ritual guidelines to use in the future and to share with others looking for insight.

Keys to Successful Ritual

By these festival rites, from the age that is past, to the age that is waiting before.

—Samuel Gilman

Successful ritual results from a combination of forethought, astute discernment, attitude, tradition, personal insight, and instinct. Forethought helps everything flow smoothly from planning to execution. This also gives the ritual planner(s) the chance to consider all the participants' needs, limitations, and magical knowledge in the way the ritual is assembled.

KEYS TO SUCCESS

1. forethought
2. astute perception
3. proper attitude
4. tradition
5. personal insight
6. instinct

Astute discernment helps the practioner(s) gather spiritually significant components, props, and so forth. These components or objects mirror the ritual's script so it can be completed successfully. They also provide symbolic, sensual input (sight, sound, aroma, etc.), which improves the ritual's impact on the participants.

Carrying the right attitude into the ritual is very important. Not every moment of a ritual needs to be stone-faced serious— but a ritual IS serious magical business. Think of this time like a metaphysical church service. It's hard to focus on significance and meaning when you're ill, out of sorts, or when the members of a group are bickering. Those types of circumstances or problems will negatively influence the magic you're trying to create. So unless it's a matter of urgency, if the right outlook seems elusive, it's best to wait for a better time.

Tradition offers a historical or cultural context to the ritual setting. Each magical group has different, customary ways of enacting rituals. From the types of robes worn to the words spoken, each element in the ritual reflects something significant about that particular metaphysical path. For example, groups with strong Celtic roots might wear robes that have knotwork edging to honor that heritage, or have a special Gaelic prayer that they recite. In the years ahead, tradition will become all the more important because it helps establish a traceable religion with firm roots to nourish it and hold it firm against persecution.

Tradition does leave room for creativity, however. Personal insight ignites that creativity, and encourages the practitioner to make meaningful adjustments to the traditional contexts. These adjustments put life and vitality into regularly repeated rites so they don't become rote dogma.

Finally, instinct inspires us to respond spontaneously to Spirit, no matter the ritual's "script." This last point is very important. There are times when Spirit uses ritual as a means of meeting a pressing need, or communicating important information, so we need to keep our inner senses open and flexible to this nudge when it comes.

Note: Due to the longer nature of rituals, only a few are included in this chapter. For more information on ritual creation and a collection of sample Wiccan rituals, consult *A Wiccan Book of Ceremonies and Rituals* (Citadel, 1998).

Seasonal Rituals

Four seasons fill the measure of the year.

—John Keats

The Wiccan wheel of the year follows the seasons to commemorate the changes in the earth reflected in nature. These rituals are the four major points on that wheel, like a crossbar that holds everything together and keeps the cycle moving. By following this pattern, this natural rhythm, we can allow the earth and the Sacred Powers to guide our way through the new millennium.

Spring Ritual

The major Wiccan spring ritual takes place on or around March 21, the Spring Equinox. This rite commemorates the earth's rebirth and the sun's return. Other themes for the observance include liberation, new beginnings, and fertility.

To prepare, gather some early blooming flowers, a pastel-colored altar cloth, and white or yellow candles for decoration. Place a cup of mulberry wine on the altar along with a small string of sweetly toned bells (or a wind chime). Burn a mixture of mint and lavender incense to emphasize spring's refreshing winds. Gather a dish of soil, seeds, a red candle, and a bowl of water for the four Quarter points, and consider wearing light, comfortable clothing that rejoices in the warmth that's returned to the planet.

Invocation

This begins in the North, to honor the earth's awakening, then moves around the circle clockwise, stopping at each Quarter point to recite one verse. If possible, enact this ritual at dawn, the hour of new beginnings.

In the North, say, "*In the beginning, the Lord and Lady danced upon the fertile earth, creating hills and valleys, plains and mountains.*" Scatter a small handful of soil here.

In the East, say "*In the beginning, the Lord and Lady scattered seed to the four winds so that the earth would flourish with beauty.*" Scatter seeds here.

In the South, say "*In the beginning, the Lord and Lady warmed the earth, shining brilliant light over the four corners of creation.*" Light a candle here.

In the West, say "*In the beginning, the Lord and Lady wept for joy over the radiance of the world, their tears becoming nourishing rains.*" Sprinkle water here.

Move to the Center and light whatever candles you've chosen to represent the Lord and Lady at your celebration. Then hold a cup of wine high to the sky saying: "*Youthful Goddess, full of happiness and play, welcome. Youthful God, full of zeal and energy, welcome.*"

Ritual

Take a sip of the wine and pour the rest to the earth. (If you're working indoors, you can pour this into a pot of soil instead and take it outside later to return the magic to the earth.) Say: "*Let the sweet wine of spring bring fertility and beauty back to the earth. Hail, Spring!*"

Replace the cup on the altar. Next, lay the strand of bells (or the wind chime) across both palms and visualize it being filled with the pale, yellow light of dawn. As you visualize, repeat this incantation: "*Ring out hope; chime with freedom. With each wind, let the magic begin!*"

At this point, consider doing the spring meditation given in chapter 3, or the spring charms and spells from chapters 4 and 5. Before closing the circle, hang up your magical chimes to ring out their power.

Closing the Circle

This begins in the West and ends in the North, again emphasizing the earth's transformation as the central point of the ritual.

In the West, say "*The rain has fallen and the earth all around has grown green. Thank you for this blessing and for protecting this sacred space. Farewell.*"

In the South, say "*The sun's fire has nourished all things, and warmth has returned. Thank you for this blessing and for protecting this sacred space. Farewell.*"

In the East, say "*The winds have scattered seeds and brought fertility. Thank you for this blessing and for protecting this sacred space. Farewell.*"

In the North, say "*The soil is filled to overflowing with life and beauty. Thank you for this blessing and for protecting this sacred space. Farewell.*"

In the Center, say *"Lord and Lady, we join with you in your dance of life; it renews our energy. Thank you for being here with us for this blessing, and the dawning of a new cycle in the earth. Farewell."* Extinguish the Lord and Lady candles.

If you wish, add the spring prayer from chapter 2 here. Make notes of your experience in a journal or discuss them over some refreshments.

Summer Ritual

The major Wiccan summer ritual takes place on or around June 21, the Summer Solstice. This rite commemorates the power of light over darkness and spiritual "fire." Other themes for the observance include love, energy, and truth.

To prepare, gather your favorite summer flowers and a red- or gold-colored altar cloth. Throughout the sacred space and at each Quarter point, place vibrant yellow, orange, or red candles. Put a cup of red vegetable juice on the altar along with a brazier (ignited) and powdered cinnamon, ginger, nutmeg, and orange peel in a separate small bowl. Get a lantern with a white candle burning inside to represent Spirit and leave this at the center of the altar. Also leave a red-colored cloth and white ribbon on the altar for each participant.

Invocation

Begin this invocation in the South to honor the fire element. If possible, enact the ritual at noon when the sun is highest in the sky.

In the South, say *"Fires of Power, Fires of Spirit, be welcome in this place. Even as the sun blazes in the sky, overpowering darkness, burn too in my heart."* Light the candle.

In the West, say *"Fires of Warmth, Fires of Love, be welcome in this place. Even as the sun warms the earth, let it also warm my heart."* Light the candle.

In the North, say *"Fires of Evolution, Fires of Progress, be welcome in this place. Even as the sun brings growth to earth's greenery, let it also nurture my heart."* Light the candle.

In the East, say *"Fires of Creation, Fire of All Beginnings, be welcome in this place. Even as the sun inspires the earth's seeds, so, too, let it inspire my heart."* Light the candle.

Ritual

Go to the altar and take the herbs placed there in hand saying, *"Burn with my prayers, burn with my wishes, hopes, and dreams."*

Sprinkle the herbs into the brazier and let them ignite. As they do, whisper a wish or prayer into the smoke that represents what you most need presently. Let this burn unhindered, carrying your magic and message.

Next, pick up the Spirit candle and, starting in the south, use it to light all the other candles placed around the room, moving clockwise as you say, *"Great One, light of lights, renew the world. Hail Summer!"*

Repeat this all the way around the circle, then return the candle to the center of the altar and take up the cup of juice. Hold it up saying, *"Ignite the embers of Spirit within me."*

Each participant should drink from the cup. The leader then pours a little of the remainder on the burning brazier saying, *"Even when the fire is extinguished, it is never really gone."*

Consider doing the summer meditation from chapter 3 at this point, and possibly the summer spell or charm in chapters 4 and 5, before closing the circle.

Closing the Circle

In the East, say *"Dawn has passed, but the light remains strong. I thank the Powers for each miracle of each new morning."* Blow out the candle.

In the North, say *"Darkness has not yet come, but the stars still shine. I thank the Powers for the beauty above, below, and all around."* Blow out the candle.

In the West, say *"Twilight is approaching, but the sun's strength has not yet waned. I thank the Powers for the ever-turning wheel that gives significance to each moment."* Blow out the candle.

In the South, say *"It is the sun's brilliant hour; the summer of life and the apex of energy. I thank the Powers for this fire, which burns ever in my heart."* Blow out the candle.

Consider adding the spring prayer from chapter 2 here. After the ritual each participant can take one red cloth, a pinch of the leftover herbal mixture, and bind it up as an charm for love, light, and renewed energy. Also give the leftover beverage to the earth by way of blessing and libation

Fall Ritual

The major Wiccan fall ritual takes place on or around September 21, the Autumn Equinox. This rite commemorates the harvest and the earth's generous gifts to us. Other themes for the observance include conservation, frugality, and sharing.

To prepare, gather apples, nuts, squash, pumpkins, grapes, and other freshly harvested edibles to decorate the circle. Use an orange-colored altar cloth dotted with fall leaves and any candles desired. Put a cup of grape wine or cider on the altar along with a Spirit candle, a handful of nuts, and a piece of black construction paper.

Invocation

This begins in the West, the region associated with fall metaphysically. Start this ritual at sunset, and if possible, place symbolic items at the four Quarters that you can pick up and hold during the invocation, like a cup of water or a shell, seeds or soil, a fan, and a candle or incense.

In the West, say *"Lady of the Waters I welcome your abundant energy. Let my heart overflow with gladness."*

In the Noth, say *"Earth mother I welcome your harvest. Let me reap seeds of character."*

In the East, say "*Lord of the Winds I welcome your changes. Let me breathe deeply the air of thoughtfulness.*"

In the South, say "*Fire Father I welcome your warm protection. Let me burn with Spirit's embers.*"

Ritual

Go to the altar and hold the cup high to the sky saying, "*Gods and Goddesses of Earth and the Harvest, you have been generous once more and now I return your kindness with a thankful heart.*"

Pour out half of the cup to the earth to return the gift given by the soil. (If you wish, put a fruit or vegetable bearing seedling in the ground here, too). Pass the cup to all participants one at a time saying, "*What is it you wish to harvest?*"

Each participant replies, "*I harvest and accept the ability to _____.*" [Fill in the blank with the characteristic or attribute desired, and take a sip.]

If you're working the ritual alone, simply skip the "what is your wish...." Replace the cup on the altar. Consider using the fall meditation from chapter 3 at this point in the ritual, and the fall spell and charm from chapters 4 and 5.

Afterward take the candle from the altar and hold it in both hands while thinking intently about one question that lies heavy on your heart (fall is a favored time for divinatory efforts). Visualize the question in symbolic or literal terms if possible. When you feel ready, tip the candle toward the black paper so the wax freely drips down saying, "*Spirit of insight, reveal the answer. Open my inner sight so I can see what you place here.*"

Let the candle keep dripping in a random pattern for three to four minutes, then replace the candle. Leave the paper to dry through the rest of the ritual; you can scry it for interpretive value later during the grounding time.

Finally, take the nuts (with the shells on) and hold both hands, palm-down, over them saying, "*Spirit of Providence, Fill! Fill! By your power, by my will!*"

Each participant should take one of these nuts home and open it only when they have a pressing need. Opening the nut releases the magic. At least one of the nuts should be planted in the earth, too, to fulfill the planet's needs.

Closing the Circle

Move counterclockwise, beginning in the East.

In the East, say "*The winds grow quiet, but the magic stays to keep me judicious and thrifty each day. Hail and farewell.*"

In the North, say "*The earth is weary, but potential remains to grant strong foundations, when the sun wanes. Hail and farewell.*"

In the West, say "*The waters chill, but house life deep within to feed the spirit, so let the wheel spin! Hail and farewell.*"

In the South, say "*The fires die down, but the coals still burn to maintain our soul, and the lessons it's learned. Hail and farewell.*"

Consider adding the fall prayer from chapter 2 here, then enjoy noting your experiences, or a time of fellowship over a Thanksgiving-styled feast!

Winter Ritual

The major Wiccan winter ritual takes place on or around December 21, the Winter Solstice (or Yule). This rite commemorates the slow return of the sun and Spirit's providence through the harsh months. Other themes for the observance include thoughtfulness, creativity, and personal well-being.

To prepare, decorate the circle with pine branches, holly, and ivy, all of which represent the power of spirit to overcome "death." The pine specifically welcomes the sylvan beings into your sacred space. Have a gold candle (to represent the sun) at the center of the altar along with a cup of wassail or eggnog. Also, have one piece of mistletoe per participant placed on the altar. Around the sacred space, place white candles dotted with silver glitter and have them lit when you begin the invocation.

Invocation

This invocation begins in the North, the region of snow and cold. If possible, begin the ritual in the dark of night.

In the North, say "*Spirits of the earth, rouse from your slumber for a moment. Shake off the blankets of snow and frost to join me in this sacred space. I honor the magical night, and welcome the returning sun.*"

In the East, say "*Spirits of the air, blow gentle from your resting place. Join me in this sacred space where in darkness, I shall find light to walk the Path of Beauty.*"

In the South, say "*Spirits of the fire, burn brightly again. While your power waned momentarily, it is time to awaken. Join me in this sacred space where warm hearts will replace winter's chill.*"

In the West, say "*Spirits of the water, break free from winter's icy grasp. Flow freely once more! Join us in this sacred space where your intuitive waves will not be hindered.*"

In the Center, light the gold candle, which represents both Spirit and the Sun, and say "*Father Fire, Mother Hearth, take strength from this candle, and come share this sacred space.*"

Ritual

As you stand before the altar, take up the cup saying, "*We are each as unique as a snowflake designed by Spirit, but even such beauty can have flaws. During this season I ask for strength and health to attend my tasks. Let me be well in body, mind, and soul.*"

Take a drink from the cup and pour the rest to the earth saying, "*May the blessings of warmth and health be likewise bestowed on the earth, our Mother.*"

Put the cup down. Take the Sun candle to begin lighting all the others in the room, moving clockwise (the natural movement of the sun). As each one ignites say, "*Strength to the Sun; strength to my heart.*" Put the Spirit candle back on the altar.

Place your hands, palms down, over the bowl of mistletoe. Close your eyes and visualize it being filled with golden-white light while saying, "*As in the days of old, I honor the magical power of the golden bough. By Apollo and Odin, and all gods and goddesses who held this plant sacred, let it be filled with healing, love, and protection this night. Whoever bears this gift is a friend of earth, so guard them well.*" Give a piece to each participant.

At this point consider adding the winter meditation from chapter 3, or a spell or charm from chapters 4 and 5.

Closing the Circle

Begin by walking counterclockwise around the circle once, blowing out half of the white and silver candles. As you walk, say, "*The sun is down. It has reached the lowest point in the sky, but it will not tarry. Hope is not lost. Even when we cannot see it, the sun is there and tomorrow it will grow strong again, as will my spirit.*"

In the East, say "*Spirit of the wind, bear away the snow. Within my heart, let the magic flow. As above, so below; with each dawn, hope bestow. So be it.*"

In the North, say "*Spirit of the earth, remain hardy and sure—within my heart, let the magic stir. As the old decays, your beauty endures—with each day, keep my intentions pure. So be it.*"

In the West, say "*Spirit of the water, flow out from the seas. Within my heart, let the magic course free. As within, so without, it's easy to see with each moment, that the magic is me. So be it.*"

In the South, say "*Spirit of the fire, burn ever, burn bright; within my heart, the magic—ignite! What once was dark, now fill with light; within me, spark inner sight. So be it.*"

Consider closing with the winter prayer from chapter 2, then enjoy traditional Yule foods. Keep your sun candle from this celebration intact. It can become the center of the Yule log or be used to light a new sun candle next year, thereby representing life's continuance. When the original candle gets too small for this, remelt its wax with some additional yellow-colored wax, and make a new one filled with all the energy of rituals past!

Thematic Ritual

In life, as in chess, forethought wins.

—Sir Thomas Buxton

The focus of this book was that of preparing ourselves and our magic for all the potentialities the future holds. Thus, the thematic ritual for this chapter is likewise centered on being prepared—making our minds, bodies, and spirits as ready as possible for all the changes to come.

To prepare for these Thematic Rituals, you'll need five anointing oils ready and waiting at the Quarter points. These can be made easily from blending a few drops of essential oil with regular olive or almond oil. If you have oily skin, mix the essentials with water or make a tea from fresh herbs instead. You won't need a lot. The five aromas and alternatives are: vetivert, patchouli, or primrose (earth/north); lavender, lemon verbena, or pine (air/east); peppermint, cinnamon, or ginger (fire/south); vanilla, coconut, or jasmine (water/west). On the altar, also have a bowl of spring water, some burning incense (any kind), and a heather branch or a feather.

Invocation

This invocation begins in the Center then moves out to emphasize the individual as the center of magic. Consider having objects or aromatics at the Quarter points that correspond to the invocation.

In the Center, say "*Great Lord and Lady, you who are without beginning or end, I welcome you. Let me hear your voices as they softly whisper to my heart, and feel your guiding power in my magic as you protect this sacred space.*"

In the South, say "*Fiery angel, Ariel, open my eyes to the beauty that is always around me, but often unappreciated. Bear the scent of flowering almonds on your coals as you protect this sacred space. So mote it be.*"

In the West, say "*Angel of the waves, Raphael, flow into this place, filling it with the scent of the sacred lotus. Let me taste your inspired waters and drink deeply of them, as you protect this sacred space. So mote it be.*"

In the North, say "*Earth angel, Gabriel, come touch my heart. Bring to this place the smell of grains growing in the earth's fields, and the energy of firm foundations as you protect this sacred space. So mote it be.*"

In the East, say "*Angel of the winds, Michael, bear the scents of primrose and violets on your breezes. Wrap your gentle wings around this place that I might grow, learn, and prepare for the future. Protect this sacred space. So mote it be.*"

Ritual

Return to the altar and pick up the heather branch or feather. Dip it into the spring water saying, "*Purify and energize; by my will, the magic fulfill!*" Whisper this phrase while sprinkling the water around you, into your aura. As you do, visualize your auric field being filled with brilliant, silver-white light that glitters like stars.

Next, go to the southern point of your circle again. Take the anointing oil in hand saying, "*With fire and light, prepare my site!*" Anoint the region of your face called the third eye, which lies on your forehead just above where your nose meets your eyes. Take a moment to meditate on the power of fire and light to chase away the shadows in your life, now and in the future.

Go to the western point of your circle. Take the anointing oil in hand, saying, "*By water and rain, intuition to gain!*" Dab this on the area over your heart. Take a moment to meditate on the way that love and insight transform and prepare us.

Go to the northern point of your circle. Take the anointing oil in hand saying, "*In soil to grow, foundations bestow!*" Dab this on your feet. Take a moment to meditate on your spiritual roots, and how they continue to nurture you.

Go to the eastern point of your circle (this way you end at the beginning). Take the anointing oil in hand saying, "*By inspiring winds I am transformed, every dawn to be reborn!*" Dab a little of this *carefully* on you eyelids. Meditate on the miracle of each new day and the opportunities every moment of living brings.

Return to the altar. Before closing the circle, whisper a wish you have for the new millennium into the smoke of the burning incense. Let this burn itself out naturally so it can carry that energy and wish to its goal. Consider adding the meditation for connecting with the Sacred here, or other favorite spells, prayers, and charms that accent the theme of foresight and change.

Closing the Circle

This closing ends in the East to emphasize how all things return to the Source, and begin again.

In the North, say *"Powers of the Earth, thank you for your presence and support. Take your leave of this sacred space, but keep your roots firm in my Path and in my heart."*

In the West, say *"Powers of the West, thank you for your presence and insight. Take your leave of this sacred space, but forever flow into my spirit and heart."*

In the South, say *"Powers of the South, thank you for your presence and energy. Take your leave of this sacred space, but forever burn in my soul and heart."*

In the East, say *"Powers of the East, thank you for your presence and awareness. Take your leave of this sacred space, but continue to breathe afresh in my heart."*

In the Center, say a heartfelt prayer or dismissal of your own making.

Children's Rituals

> Where children are, there is the golden age.
>
> —Novalis

Children's rituals are generally shorter than adult ones and have a lighter atmosphere. These rites give children an opportunity to stretch their attentive skills, and their spirits, by creatively interacting with the metaphysical world (guided by an adult). Whenever possible, the children involved should themselves call the Quarters (and other terms) so they learn how to work with magical energy more effectively.

Sometimes it helps to present this idea to the children as taking a role in a special play. Explain to them the importance of this "play" and what to expect in advance. Then, walk the children through a few "dress rehearsals" so they feel comfortable with the proceedings. In the end, as children get older, this prepares them for taking on an adult role in your family circles.

Animal Guide

Most children have a natural affinity for animals. This ritual is designed to help them find a personal animal guide that can stay with them and support them through the most difficult parts of growing up.

You'll need a small piece of bread, a celery leaf, seeds, and a bowl of water for each child. These are left on the altar until needed. You also need one nine-inch strand of yellow yarn for each child participating.

Invocation

Rhyming invocations help children remember them better. Older children can write some of their own. This particular invocation ends in the North to emphasize the earth and its creatures. If possible, enact the circle outdoors—it proves far more successful.

In the East, say "*Lord of the Wind come dance and play—join us in this sacred space today.*"

In the South, say "*Lord of the Fires, warm us within, so our magic can begin.*"

In the West, say "*Lady of Water, fill us with cheer—cleanse and protect everyone here.*"

In the North, say "*Lady of Earth, reveal your spirits—let them join in this circle with us.*"

The Ritual

Have each child take the seeds, celery, bread, and a bowl of water to a spot in the circle, facing outward. Have them pour out the water, sprinkle the seeds, break the bread, and toss the celery leaves out to the ground saying, "*Spirit animals of water, earth, air, and fire, take our gifts, our dreams inspire!*"

Next, give each child the yellow yarn. Have them tie into it three knots saying, "*With the knot of one, my magic's begun. With the knot of two, let my dreams be true. With the knot of three, bring my guide to me!*"

Every night for the next three days the children should keep the yarn knots under their pillow and a dream journal handy. If a spirit animal is to come, it will reveal itself in these dreams.

Closing the Circle

The circle will close in the North to honor the earth again.

In the West, say "*Waves and rain, waves and rain, merry part and merry meet again.*"

In the South, say "*Fire and flame, fire and flame, return freely from where you came.*"

In the East, say "*Air and wind, wind and air, move our power, our magic bear.*"

In the North, say "*Earth and stone, earth and stone, stay with us till we're safely home.*"

Take time after the ritual to let the children discuss the experience and verbalize what they think different animals might represent (and why).

My Soul Is a Tree

Since children represent our spiritual future, it's important that they become aware of themselves as spiritual beings. This ritual is designed to improve that awareness, and impart growing strength to a child's soul.

You'll need a small token, chosen by the child to represent himself, and a hair or nail cutting. This ritual has to take place outdoors where there are several healthy trees that aren't likely to be disturbed (a park is a good choice).

Invocation

This invocation will begin in the East, to mark the beginning of an improved relationship with the earth for the children.

In the East, say "*Spirit of the Elm, Palm, and Aspen tree, come, share this sacred space with me.*"

In the South, say "*Spirit of the Oak, Ash, and Bay, come, be with us on this special day!*"

In the West, say "*Spirit of the Apple, Birch, and Yew, Come with your magic, our spirits—renew!*"

In the North, say "*Spirit of the Honeysuckle and Primrose join in; by your power and our will let the magic begin.*"

Ritual

Have each child take her token and clippings in hand and look around. Have them close their eyes for a moment and listen intently for the voice of one tree calling to them. They should go to whatever tree to which they feel drawn and place their tokens in the earth below it saying, "*My soul is this tree, strong and sure, and growing always toward the light.*"

The child should spend a few minutes with the tree to "get to know it." They can visit their soul tree any time they wish to give it little gifts, water it, tend it, or what have you. As they do, they also tend their own spirit! Note: If the tree ever looks sickly, if the child moves away, or if the tree is in danger of being dug up, the tokens should be removed.

Finally, have the child gather a small branch from this tree that he can fashion later into a personal wand. He can wrap wire around it, paint it, glue on crystals and feathers—whatever he wishes—then point it to direct magical power during rituals and spells.

Closing the Circle

In the North, say "*Farewell, Northern tree spirits, be free! Thank you for your strong roots and company.*"

In the West, say "*Farewell, Western tree spirits, be free! Thank you for your inspiration and company.*"

In the South, say "*Farewell, Southern tree spirits, be free! Thank you for your energy and company.*"

In the East, say "*Farewell, Eastern tree spirits, be free! Thank you for knowledge and company.*"

Take time afterward to discuss why children picked a particular tree, how they felt about the ritual, and what they experienced

Earth-Healing Ritual

Study nature as the countenance of God.

—Charles Kingsley

Every day should be earth day in the way we act toward the planet. Unfortunately, many of us get so busy that we forget to walk gently on this planet that we steward. Earth-healing rituals, therefore, are designed as a magical salve to fill in some of those gaps in time and space with powerful, spiritual energy that protects and heals.

Begin by finding an outdoor location for the rite. Use natural, fallen greenery to mark and decorate the sacred space. On the altar have a cup of spring water, a bowl of seeds, burning incense, and a handful of feathers (you can obtain these at a craft store).

Invocation

This invocation appeals to the earth's elements and elementals (the beings that abide in a specific element-medium) for help in healing the planet.

In the East, say "*Winds whose breath gives life to all creatures, come be my guide. Protect this sacred space and activate my magic.*"

In the South, say *"Fires whose warmth maintains and cleanses all things, come be my guide. Protect this sacred space and energize my magic."*

In the West, say *"Waters whose waves inspire and heal all things, come be my guide. Protect this sacred space and purify my magic."*

In the North, say *"Earth whose soils sustain us and grant life, come be my guide. Protect this sacred space and give roots to my magic."*

In the Center, say *"Great spirit, whose power abides within and without all things, come be my guide. Protect this sacred space and give life to my magic."*

Ritual

Go to the altar and take the feathers in hand. Stand facing the eastern Quarter, visualize the feathers being filled with pale yellow light and say, *"I release the power of air to carry transformation and healing to the land and all living things."* Release the feathers to carry the magic.

Take the incense in hand. Stand facing the southern Quarter, visualize the smoke being filled with pale red light and say, *"I release the power of fire to burn away pollution and warm the land and all living things with clean energy."* Blow on the smoke so that it streams out in all directions, carrying the magic.

Take the water in hand. Stand facing the western Quarter and visualize the water being filled with pale bluish-purple light and say. *"I release the power of water to cleanse, inspire, and give hope to the land and all living things."* Pour the water to the ground so it saturates the soil with magic.

Take the seeds in hand. Stand facing the northern Quarter and visualize them being filled with rich brown and green light saying, *"I release the power of earth to nurture and sustain the land and all living things."* Scatter the seeds to the soil so magic takes root.

Finally, consider adding any of the earth-healing meditations, spells, or charms at this point in the proceedings.

Closing the Circle

This closing ends in the North to focus all your magic toward the traditional earth-center.

In the West, say "*The waters recede, yet their dews remain to feed each root and creature, making them whole. So, too, feed my soul. Hail and farewell.*"

In the South, say "*The fires die down, yet their warm coals remain to sustain and energize all things. So too warm my heart. Hail and farewell.*"

In the East, say "*The winds calm, yet the air remains to breathe new life and hope into all things. So, too, give hope to my mind. Hail and farewell.*"

In the North, say "*The earth rests, yet the seeds remain fertile to bring new life to all things as the wheel turns. So, too, give new life to my spirit. Hail and farewell.*"

End with one of the earth-healing prayers from chapter 2. Then, sit down where you are and talk about (or write about) how it feels to be close to nature. Extend all your senses to really become "one" with the earth, and appreciate that unity. Carry that feeling with you so that each time you touch a plant, or walk on the soil, you can return some positive energy to the world that so generously sustains us.

New Millennium Ritual

> Time is the chrysalis of eternity.
>
> —J. P. Richter

Since the new millennium technically starts at 12:01 A.M. 2001, this ritual is designed to begin just before midnight on December 31, 2000. The idea is to usher in a new age with potent, meaningful magic. It can be performed any time, however, or any New Year thereafter to sustain the magic's power long into the future.

To begin you'll need a new ritual robe (or clothing), an hourglass, and a cup of water on the altar, along with an image of the past (with a lit candle before it), and a positive image of the future (with an unlit candle before it), at opposite sides of the ritual space. Decorate the area with silver and gold confetti, streamers, balloons, and traditional New Year's highlights. The silver-and-gold scheme represents the yin-yang, moon-sun, intuitive-logical balance of energies necessary for successful spiritual living.

Invocation

This invocation features the gods and goddesses who preside over destiny and the future as guides for the magic you're creating.

In the East, say "*Fa, god of destiny, come to me! Weave time's web insightful. Fashion the future with the breath of life and hope.*"

In the South, say "*Janus, who both past and future sees, come to me! Shine a light on the shadows, banish the darkness, and grant a tomorrow where your vision is a guide.*"

In the West, say "*Cardea, goddess of the ever-turning wheel, come to me! Bring with your motion a new year filled with the waters of understanding and healing.*"

In the North, say "*Strenia, goddess of the new year, come to me! As the clock strikes twelve, empower the new millennium with magic.*"

In the Center, say "*Great Spirit, who is all, and in whom all are one, come to me! Let the new year be filled with your light and love, within and without.*"

Ritual

Move to the region of the circle where you placed the symbol of the past. Take the candle before it saying, "*The past creates the future—it lights our way with lessons learned. Let the wisdom of our yesterdays illuminate our tomorrows.*"

Take the past's candle to the symbol of the future and light the candle in front of the emblem saying, "*The past is never forgotten, but now we must look forward. Let the light of love, peace, and truth be in my mind and heart.*" Consider adding a meditation here.

Take up the cup of water saying, "*As water is shaped by what holds it, so do I know that the future is shaped by my hands. I accept this responsibility and pledge to do all I can to make every day a little better than the last.*" Pour out the water to the earth.

At midnight go to the altar and turn over the hourglass saying, "*The sands of time; the changing fates; tomorrow is here; forever is now. Let me build a better tomorrow; let me become one with the future and destiny.*"

Change your clothing to reflect the changing times. If desired, add prayers, charms, and spells at this point.

Closing the Circle

This closing is recited while the leader slowly turns counter-clockwise at the center of the circle, with outstretched arms, to dismiss the Powers. (This creates a visual image of a clock face moving backward with the leader at center.)

In the North, say "*Strenia, the page of time has turned; the wheel has turned. Thank you for escorting the new year in safely, for grounding it in rich soil to root and mature, and for protecting this sacred space.*"

In the West, say "*Cardea, the old year is gone; we honor what is past and what is yet to come. Thank you for turning the wheel toward a tomorrow filled to overflowing with blessings, and for protecting this sacred space.*"

In the South, say "*Janus, the door of time swings upon its hinge. Thank you for lighting the way to the future with yesterday's lessons, and for protecting this sacred space.*"

In the East, say "*Fa, the dawn of a new era has come, and with it we meet our destiny with hopeful hearts. Thank you for this new beginning and for protecting this sacred space.*"

Do things after the circle that will promote happiness, health, and prosperity in the future. Eat rich foods, make peace with family and friends, and fellowship with those you love.

Final Reflections

I cannot help but hope for a better future for my children—a future that we have created from life-affirming magic. But the real magic is not in words, cookie-cutter procedures, nor any number of spells cast. It comes from living our lives in a uniquely thoughtful, spiritual way each day. If we do this dilligently, then our future will indeed be bright, exciting, and filled with the miracles that come from mutual respect, unconditional love, and global peace.

Keep hope in your heart!